NAKED

Vicente Moreno Martin

Copyright @ 2006
Vicente Moreno Martin

All rights reserved. No part of this book
may be reproduced, without the permission
in writing from the author.
ISBN
978-0-6151-8090-8
Printed by lulu.com

PROLOGUE
Kyoto, Japan-15 February 2006

When I published 'A DREAM CATCHER', I thought that so many of my friends, like the reduced numbers of readers that could read it, would accept it as a gift, without demanding explanations. But it was not so.

The first surprised was myself, when to read it all over again, already published, I discovered in it a manual of perfection.

The author is the primary beneficiary of the book. It has been I, the one learning the most, not only when I read it yet again, but when receiving the observations and investigations of the people.

Moreover, through chatters and presentations, I penetrate into a psychological point, unknown, previously, by me.

For a counted number of people, 'A dream catcher', has been a door of entrance to a world, for them unknown. And I find myself repaid if only has reached to wake up the heart of a human being.

Those who know me more, consider that I have discovered myself in front of the world, and they see me naked. It was not my primordial interest. But everyone demands an explanation from me. So this book is an answer to those questions.

I perceive our humanity as a cluster of souls in evolution, to whom I designate as 'brothers', because we belong to the same family.

We are offered, to work in this one physical world, a mind, which is our instrument of work, a hoe to dig the earth.

In the description, marvelously written in Genesis, Adam is our spirit, Eve our mind. Eve is our help, to the service of Adam.

When Eve-mind refuses the guiding principle of Adam-spirit and trusts in the external information-snake, becomes dazzled with this material world, consumes it and offers its food to the spirit.

When the intimacy swallows the superficial world, flees from oneself, observes his nakedness, he is ashamed and hides from God.

To assume the supremacy of the material over the psychic, is to exile oneself from Paradise.

If you want to return to it, dear

friend, you have to know yourself, detach manually from all clothes you have covered yourself with, do not follow the suggestions of the mind, but trusts in the Intuition, channel your Way towards the house of the Father, and return to Paradise, to the mansion, of the one that you went away from.

But you will find the entrance to it, blocked by a Seraph, a Snake of fire, with whom you will have to meet face to face.

The spiritual guides, our brothers, have come to help us, giving us feelings of hope to continue in our task, which is private and common, since we all are part of a same humanity.

From the beginning of the human history, we have entered a channel to work physically; constructing Empires and material glories', accepting beliefs to attain immortality, or eternal honor.

We are ourselves the same ancient inhabitants of the archaic Empires, returning once and again. We are the identical residents that build up those Temples and Palaces.

As all the civilizations were and are founded with the mental or physical labor, they enclose in themselves the seed of destruction, and they collapse turning into powder.

The Art, being a fruit of our feelings, remains, in this planet, as a footprint of our perceptions. And, being fragile, in the Architecture, Sculpture, Painting, Music, persists the feeling of the artists, if we achieve to pierce into the alchemy of their breath.

In the ether of our world we find engravings of all our acts, small that they may be. Nothing gets lost in creation.

The life itself presents them to us, daily, for our reconsideration.

If you search for your own inside quietness, in it appears, suddenly, in order that you may rethink them and acquire wisdom.

The pages of our history are, as well, flooded with rulers, pharaohs, emperors and kings, that with their eagerness of greatness they have distress our simple evolution, in a heap of personal repercussions resurfacing without an end.

If we acknowledge that the human being is eternal and we reborn once and again, these sequels of love and hate descry to us as persistent.

The Teacher came to instruct us to stop our mind, led to the abyss, and make a turn of course, in our painful ascension.

We have not yet given Him any attention.

In the current world we value only the pronouncements of our intelligence and nullify our feelings, or we cover our conscience with 'family' and exclusive morals, which they are opposed to a universal feeling.

Those who have developed the brain get material power and they self-proclaim themselves masters and guides of the rest of the people, presenting to our unconcerned humanity, a world completely fictitious, imaginary and unreal.

It is already late in our exit from this planet towards other superior orbs, and the animal world is waiting for our advancement, to occupy the place that belongs to them.

We undergo symptoms of asphyxia when observing every one of our brothers trying to save their own 'I', without any concern for the commonwealth.

I encounter in my daily life seconds of clarity, in which I see vaguely a glorious universe, but after this instant, I observe the violence of our society, increasingly grotesque and crude, that with its fist of lead, it flattens any human ideal counteracting its low selfish interests.

I cannot force the evolution of any human being; neither can I load any of them on my shoulders. It has to be you, beloved friend, the one which set out your Way, if is it what you want.

This is a road of Light, Love, and Freedom. And with Light, more Light, with Love more Love and with Freedom more Freedom... and all these... endless.

Return to your heart and search in your inside for your own wisdom.

If today you listen to His voice, harden not your heart.

When you begin to discover what is inside you, and launch to remove your own pretexts, you will observe your world more attractive that any exterior entertainment.

Scratch your heart a little and you will find there a source that sprouts for all eternity. Drink from it, and it will satisfy your thirst, giving you strength and energy until you reach your goal. Do not search for it outside of you, since you would not discover it. May it clean out your wounded feet and, like balm, protect them to continue in your arduous ascension.

God observes what hides in the soul, and this is the only delivery that He accepts: the one of your Spirit, your Freedom and your Truth.

The letters of this book do not enclose any value. Take from them their intimacy, if you may find it.

All my love to you.

NAKED

In my first book, beloved friend, I wrote to you some of my soul experiences, thinking they may be useful to you.

In your e-mail you did inform me that you read it and you do not understand it and you ask me for an explanation.

This book is a collection of common conversations and feelings happened to me recently.

The reality of the spirit cannot be entrusted in writing. There is not a law impeding it. What it happens is an order of Jesus: 'Do not tell anyone that I am the Messiah'.

The intruding is paid back with spiritual dumbness, for many years. Therefore I have a little fear when publishing these conversations.

Our personal development directs each one of us to know ourselves and to remove our spiritual apparel, the one we have accumulated for many years as our private possession. The clothing is all our mental knowledge.

We remove it, gelds to geld, resembling a Russian doll, until reaching to the tiny one, and when we open it, we only find air or spirit. Then you know the Messiah, the Savior of the World.

I tell you about Him because He is the Way, the Teacher. His work is a magisterial diagram I invite you to follow. In Him all is perfect.

I would not like to inform you about it, so as to follow the suggestion of the Teacher. It would make me very happy if you discovered it by yourself beyond the letters and of the paper.

With the desire of sharing my feelings with yours, I overtake the task to refer you my Way.

FIRST CANTICLE

FINDING FREEDOM

THREE
DOORS OF ENTRANCE

THE UNKNOWN PERSON

In a remote time, many centuries ago, on a cloudy and cold day, when I was nineteen years old, I went for a dip.

A small brook came down from the hill mixing its cold water with the small sources of thermal springs sprouting everywhere. One of them formed, just at the side of the river, a small natural Jacuzzi. The place was deserted.

I undressed and entered into the hot water. The millions of cells in my body opened in thanksgiving, and the tenderness of the flesh relaxed my mind, and I did not want to hear from anything. A few minutes later, I got out of the puddle and plunged into the cold waters. It was not only my spirit, the one that benefited from it, but my flesh, shouting out with contentment.

Immediately I returned to the hot perforation. What happiness I found in this planet! For me, to dip myself was the perfection, the greatest thing that can be experimented on this earth.

Suddenly I listen to a voice behind my back, an older man, slim and hairy, is removing his clothes to enter my same Jacuzzi.

I look around to see if there are more people, but we are the only ones in there.

- Why has this person selected my same pond, when the rest of them all are abandoned? I thought in my innermost self.

The unknown person bended his head nodding, asking permission and he seated in front of me, almost chafing my skin, but without touching me.

I was forced to watch his hairy legs and his big feet, beautiful and bony like those of a great walker. To me, he did not have any special attraction.

He looked at me.

He placed his gaze on me, and without me knowing neither why or when or how, making good use of my calm and internal silence, all of me opened to the Infinite, he placed in me an irritating particle.

It generated in me such an annoyance that I got out of the puddle, dressed myself and ran away, returning home.

It was like I was an oyster, and when opening placidly my shell, this man had grafted a small and strange pebble. Just as the oyster, I wanted to expel it from me, but

I could not, by any means, extract it.

This strange man set in me a particle crashing inside me, I wanted to force it out, but could not achieve it.

It was so, that this atom removed all my being; and my internal snake, asleep since the beginning of creation, began to disturb me violently.

All my being was in complete boiling, like a labyrinth been reorganized, like thousands of soldiers changing position, with an inside fire wasting away all my old possessions.

This pebble is the desire of God.

As well as the oyster, I began to cover this particle with substances of my being so it would not ache so much.

With time, the tiny cobblestone became a pearl.

But... how much pain and suffering. It makes me exclaim, just as Saint Theresa:

- Already I see, God, why You have so few friends, if You treat all of them as You deal with me.

In those remote times, I went away rushing, and without thinking, in an instant, I placed myself in the service of God. But for me, in that preterit antiquity, the Emperor was God, and I located myself to the service of the Emperor. Serious error, such as one I lament a lot. Even today, when reflecting on it, I could not imagine me so stupid.

With time, after many lives, I began to distinguish them.

Nowadays, staring at humanity, it seems to me the majority of the people are still worse that I was. They think that the emperor, the king, the president, the actor or the actress, the beautiful people, athletes, champions, those who acquire money and power, are gods.

Even the children ask of the religious ministers:

- Are you God?

The immaturity of the childhood refuses to disappear from our religious manners, and we confuse the Divine with the Human. Would that, although the people say that they believe in God, they have no faith. If people may say "yes", they lie; if they may say "not", they wander.

My archaic notion, of fossilized times, today becomes crueler and despot, grafting God with human concepts He does not possess. He is just, but not merciless as we are.

The man, who seated close to me and gazed at me, that one kept God above all things. I did not know his name.

Farther on, in subsequent incarnations, I have turned to see him, coming to me unexpectedly, when I was resting. The human history knows Him as Elijah or John the Baptist. He, from remote times, has been my instructor.

The Teacher Jesus says of him: 'human history does not know anyone greater than John the Baptist'.

I have read a quantity of books of records, and in all of them I could not find John.

The narrations we learn in school are a heap of politicians, and warlords, and in that gossip we do not find John.

Naturally, if you stumble in education learning actions related with your nation, you do not hear about him.

But if you transcend the books of the infancy, you mat discover the memories of the human spirit: from the prehistory, the big civilizations of Asia, of the Middle East, of the Americas, of Greece, the eagerness of development and the search for light, then you discover a new history.

In this saga of the human spirit, we are all incarnating repeatedly and living experiences in our progress towards the Illumination.

And the stories, stared at from this point of sight, are completely different. Is not what Pizarro did, but where is Pizarro now?

The file begins to acquire lucidity, of

victim it turns vivacious and you notice the great human beings, or those whom we take as such, as part of the humanity, the majority of them living in the flesh, trying to find that one key of access to the Infinite.

In the history of my spirit I discovered John the Baptist. With accuracy the human diaries had not anyone greater than he.

- Do not the people say that Elijah has to return? They ask the Teacher.

- Elijah has already come, and have done with him what they wanted, answers Jesus making reference to John the Baptist; and the one who has ears to listen may understand.

In those remote times, thousands of years ago, he presented himself in front of me, sat at my side and stared at me. I do not know how he made it, but he grafted into my soul the desire of God.

In other lives, I have lived, I have seen him, again, staring at me, and once more gazing at me with greater love than ever. Without saying a word, I have heard the Voice crying out in the desert of my soul, shouting loudly:

- Prepare in your spirit a Way towards God. Throw down all those gods you have in your mind as if they were mountains, and raise towards the surface so many human beings living flattened by the oppression of the powerful. May all mountains be packed down and all valleys be raised. You must build in your soul a straight Way of access to God.

The gospel points out, speaking of John, that, many people came to him from countless parts of the world.

What he did for me, he also prepared for thousands and thousands of human beings.

Piercing through many incarnations, minute after minute, one individual human being after another, this personality we call John, has sat in front of us and has glimpsed at us. Without a sound, his Voice has touched our inside and has transformed us.

The human history has not yet anyone as greater as John, which has loved God above all.

The people of the Old Testament hoped for a great prophet with all the pomp and the glory, an Elijah returning with his chariot of fire, and when they saw John, they despised him, and played with him, as they wanted.

He finished his life cycle on a jail, imprisoned in the obscurity, without water or sun, decapitated and hated by the powerful; the wimp of a dancer beheaded him.

Even though human history has no one greater than he, what will make with us the ephemeral man's fable?

The same incident would occur if the Teacher would return to earth. The people would say: 'this one is such a little thing', and they would despise him just as they denied John and as they relegate the many prophets God sends us constantly.

PIQUER

When I published my first book, thinking it will be the only one I would print, I went to my birth place: Algemesi, Valencia, Spain, and presented it to a group of people, whom to my surprise, received it better than I had speculated.

I gave a copy to Piquer, my friend of infancy.

Months later we got together again and he tells me that he understands nothing, that is boring... but he promised me that he is going to read it.

During the night, we went out to dine with his spouse Concha, and we were conversing a little.

- When I was three years old, I tell him, my family moved to Carrer Moli. They sat me at the door of our home. When raising my eyes, I saw you, of my same age, and we started playing in the middle of the street. We spend many summers together in Agres, exploring mountains and clearing the way for the spirit.

- I have a vague memory, Piquer answers me.

- He does not even remember the birthday of his children, comments his wife.

- On a visit to Japan some time ago, I begin to recount him; I had sights of a previous life, based on personal experience there.

'I saw me, and you at my side, and I understood that the encounter when we were three years old was not casual, but we had something in common. I am trying to explain you all these things because I have a desire to encourage you to search within yourself for that one Light of Infinite hovering over you.'

'You both, I continue, showed me with pleasure, the bonsai you bought for the first anniversary of your wedding. Is there not in your intimate memories a little more to remind you of Japan? Have you forgotten all those experiences and find them so distant looking, like if they were from another planet or humanity? How would I, as Socrates said, be able to help you to beget these recollections! But I notice myself impotent as trying to open my spirit and reveal you a new world, which possibly is not of your interest.'

- Look! My friend answers, I go to Mass every Sunday, I try to be good, and I do not criticize you, but rather I encourage you to continue writing, but these things remain far distant to me.

- For years, I continue, I had a constant image in my soul. Many times I saw myself, a small child, with short trousers, next to my home in Carrer Moli, watching the sunset at the end of the street. It was a yellowish and autumnal twilight, grandiose and melancholic.

'And during the nights, in the loneliness of the search, in Central or South America, I abandoned my soul, losing myself on the yellow imprint healing the purple marks of my spiritual blows.'

- This is because you have a gift from God, my friend ponders, you do remember almost all, and you are special.

- What special for nothing! I protest. We all are equal. I am telling you first these childhood stories because I want to encourage you to search within yourself for the spirit. And you must employ your time seeking for the missing link misplaced in your infancy.

'When we reincarnate, we encounter a concentration of experiences of past lives in the first years of our existence. In my history, like in yours, it is synthesized my pilgrimage on this planet. There is nothing "casual" in our childhood friendliness or hates, since they are consistent with previous behaviors, we catch in each life, and so we may acquire the necessary tools for our work.'

'Each night my father narrated to me fairy tales and I always demanded of him new and different fables. And my dad composed, from the many stories he read, descriptions affordable to my intelligence.'

'The world of the fairies and witches, of the development of the soul, molded in fantastic and perfect stories, revolted in my presence with more life than the daily routine of eating, drinking and working, and they broke the monotony of my days, with clear visions of the advancement of the spirit.'

'I spend my childhood days wanting them to move closer to the night so I could take note of new adventures. And my father drove into despair because his fairy tales were as long as those of Scheherazade in "A thousand and one night".'

'Already an adult, I understood Sleeping Beauty as being our soul, waiting for the Blue Prince to wake her up with a soft kiss; Cinderella is our mind, dirtied by her physical labors, but during the nights she escapes to dance with her Prince or spirit; a witch has led Sleeping Beauty to forget; Snow White, the soul, has to wake up and remember; she buries deep inside surrounded by seven little dwarfs, or vital forces; the Ugly Duckling are we, incarnated as children, in this material reality, but when we develop intimately we transform ourselves into beautiful Swans; Pinocchio is the wood, or the flesh, striving for the spirit.'

'The physical world was connected perfectly with the spiritual. And I remember, when we were nine, on the third day of Easter, we went to Ramon Diego's manor house to eat 'the Easter cake'.'

'We were seven children; and it began to rain and we shelter in his country house, and we decided to spend the night in there, but, of two and three, you all left except Ramon Diego and myself.'

- I remember vaguely your accident, and your recovery, but nothing else, he asserts.

- Already dark, it stopped raining, and we got ready to sleep on a few old sacs piled in the corner, when someone called at the door.

'With an atrocious fear, we open it, and in front of us appeared an old woman, wearing only black and with two teeth that jumped out of her mouth. She was the housekeeper, inhabiting a corner of the building. She recognized Ramon Diego, and invited us for supper.'

'The old woman lived with a child of our age, blond, with blue eyes; to the one, she commanded to go and buy wine. Ramon Diego and I accompanied him.'

'We took hours, going and coming in the darkness. I felt secure at the side of this infant I never saw before nor never will see again; a Gypsy lad, speaking to me of a world even more wonderful than my own; an angel of light displaying for me, in the darkness, the curative virtues of certain plants, of spirits of his relatives guiding him... and afterwards, when we returned to the country house, the old woman struck him with such fury, for taking such a long time, that she left him all splashed in blood.'

'With his bloodstained face, we sat to eat one only dish: some boiled fava beans, the child did steal, previously, from a neighboring field.'

'Suddenly, Ramon Diego's brother burst in where we were, shouting at us because people from the whole town were searching for us, all annoyed because he had to go to a party, and his father had ordered him to pick up his brother.'

'The accident... and only I came out wounded.'

- You see, says Piquer, of your recount, I have not even a tiny idea.

- And you remember all that? Concha questions inquisitively.

- During the months of recovery, I continue, I only thought of the Gypsy child, living with the old lady.

'I searched later on, in my life, for the friendship of the gypsies, as somewhat dearly loved.'

'I have valued more, the feelings emanating from each human experience, that the physical pain incident.'

'And I begin reporting to you stories of the infancy because first it appears as what is material and later on to what is spiritual.'

'What is initial in our life are the ancient personal experiences lived, and they are the germ of our psychic development. In them you have to construct your own existence of the soul.'

'But, if you behave like the rest of humanity, and begin to study things, so pretty and so apparently compact, adapting your life to 'outside knowledge', all what you build will be as assembling your house on sand, thrown down with each storm that flogs it.'

- Good, says Piquer to finish the conversation, please, write, truly, all of this, because I promise you that I am going to read it and to think about what you are trying to tell me.

- Give me a strong embrace, says Concha, because we both are fond to be your friends.

SEMSEM

The day was extremely hectic. When returning to the hotel, late in the afternoon, I asked for a massage appointment.

They gave it to me at 6:30pm: the last of the day.

- You may swim and rest until it is your turn, said the room clerk.

On the fixed time I arrived to the hall of massages.

- You may leave on your bathing suit, says the masseur, here in Egypt you do not need to remove it.

I stretched down on the small table, and immediately I felt his hot hands, burning when touching my skin.

He began with the feet. His fingers were trying to connect with deep nerve centers, fixing themselves in places unknown to me.

I have received several massages along my life, but this one was the only one made by a male.

With strength, he wanted to activate

my sleeping nerve centers, and as if searching to open a safe deposit box, he ascended from the feet reinforcing the muscles, and pressing each button he found, seeking for the body to open.

When he arrived to the upper part of the thigh, cautiously, he drew back towards the feet; this time, hiding again the entire compartment for him opened.

He continued afterwards with my hands, arms and torso, reaching the head. And again, to finish, he returned from the head to the hands, veiling again what he showed before.

- That's it! He says just exactly half an hour from the beginning.

- A lot of thanks, I answer, you have shaped me, besides a mixture of pleasure with ache, with an internal activity, unknown before by me.

The masseur smiles as an answer.

- You have been very cautious not to touch, not even one of the cells covered with my bathing suit, I tell him smiling.

- Those internal and personal energies have to be released only by you and I cannot help you.

- Are you pleased with the Arabs? He questions me suddenly.

- All the peoples capture me, I affirm, and the only thing I find in them all, as in the Arabs, is astounding.

- Why have you come to the massage? Were you tired? How was your day? He chases questioning.

- Tired, I answer, resolving a small problem I had with the air passage; afterwards I entered into the Egyptian Museum, and I am so tired, I want to go to sleep.

- Have you ever visited the Sphinx? He inquires.

- Yes, yesterday I went to see it.

- And what is your opinion?

- It is so huge and majestic, I manifest, but I do not know what to tell you, because the things I see have in me a retarded effect, and possibly it will take a long time, even months, to ascertain what it represents to me.

- And the Pyramids? He pursues asking.

- Incredibly beautiful and magnetic. I attain the tiny one, and I bear already two days as if the world was loaded on my shoulders. To me, the Pyramid has reduced the planet to a tiny pebble and I see it all so distant and imperceptible, weighting me down in a crushing form.

The masseur smiles cheerfully.

- I sat for hours to see the Sphinx, he adds. She changes her face constantly, and speaks and dialogues with me. It is a living being. The pyramids also have life in themselves, they were centers of initiation. The tombs are in the Valley of the Kings. Some people opine that they were not made by the Egyptians, but by extraterrestrials.

- I have a friend, Joe is his name. I can tell that he is enthused with the Ancient Egypt. We were an afternoon, watching a program about a pyramid, and he started laughing at the archaeologists while telling me:

- What nonsense! The entrance is not nearby. The threshold is found far from there, as to a few four-hundred meters. It is necessary to dig deeper to find the door. I myself took part in its construction.

'This friend, I continue, reads to me Egyptian papyruses, and explains to me the images, and I would like to come to Egypt with him to see what he discovers with his presence.'

- You invite me to join in the expedition, adds the masseur.

- Therefore I consider that they were not the extraterrestrials, I say, but us. The religious culture of the whole world springs up from the stellar knowledge, and the people wants to mix up this cosmic sight with extraterrestrials, although in certain measure, and when seeing so much destruction around us, many feel themselves from out of the planet rather than human.

- Where are you from? He asks me.

- From a small village of Valencia, in Spain.

- From Spain? I have many Spanish friends and that is where I want to go.

- The conversation is lengthening, I tell him. Do you have any more clients?

- No, he subtracts, you are the last one.

- Is there someone waiting for you, or do you want to come and have dinner? I ask.

- No one is holding me, but the regulations of the hotel forbid me to enter the restaurants, so I cannot accompany you.

- Good, so I remain with you, I tell him, because your conversation is far more interesting than supper.

- Are you from here, from Cairo? I pry.

- Yes, he indicates.

- And for how long are you working as a masseur? I continue inquiring.

- Already it goes for seven years, he responds. I was three in the Sinai. Do you know it?

I answer him that I did not.

- But it was something in the

environment I did not like, so I returned to Cairo, and I am near my family.

- What did you do before being a masseur?

- I am a mathematician, he adds. I am enchanted by mathematics. For me all are numbers, even when I do massages, I count the muscles, and I do not perceive veins nor other internal organism, but digits and codes. Do you know that we, Arabs, were the ones who invented the numbers?

- I know that you are very good with them, I corroborate.

- The people do not understand us when they go to the market, and are offered the merchandise with a price, and they have to bargain and go down with it, and many have the attitude of all of it being ill. But just imagine well, he continues saying. Who has given it the price? The value of an object is different for each one of the individuals working on it: the one who dig out the metal from underground, the one who solidified it in plates that could easily be managed, the welder shaping the vase, the engraver with the chisel, the transporter, the seller.

'What is its price? He follows up saying. Its price is hollowness. The one who sells it is trying on finding out what value this object has for you and how much you can reach to pay for it. The Arab art is the harmony between the supply and demand, between the numbers. What is important is not to sell or to buy, what is of interest is the harmonization between the purchaser and the seller; it is to search for a middle line between the two realities: this one is the Arab teaching.'

'For us, all are numbers and the mathematics is the only science of the truth.'

'We, Arabs, are more intelligent than the remainder of the peoples, because we reflect more, our philosophy goes deeper, and our way of living is a more pleasant life.'

He talks with a soft and tender voice, denoting a very affectionate soul.

- You are the third Egyptian surprising me today, I tell him.

- Why? He inquires.

- I am discovering something never before experienced by me. During the morning I went to the travel agency to solve the difficulty with the air passage, and the young man welcoming us was so sweet of character, it appeared I was in another planet.

'Afterwards, before entering the Egyptian Museum, the entrance guard tested my body with his hands. It was as if he had no hands, I almost did not notice it, such was his fineness.'

'And now you, speaking to me so smoothly, your voice reaches my soul.'

He smiles.

- Are you married? I renew my investigation.

- No, but my mother insists me daily. I am already twenty-six years old, and it is getting late for me, but precisely am working to earn money and take a trip, and go to Spain.

- Why Spain? I ask him.

- It is a long history. Are you tired or do you want me to tell you? He insinuates with a soft voice.

- I am relaxed after your massage, so I have all night ahead of me, I answer.

We sit near a table, at the side of the swimming pool, I still have my bathing suit and he has a masseur gown on. He begins to give me his point of view on history.

- I know the great human population is not worried whatsoever about their personal development, he comments, or do the great human beings starting currents of thought concern them.

'The majority of the people place their belief in a philosophical or religious ideology, they become fanatical about it, and they believe that outside of it there is not liberation.'

'Do you know that the Jewish

religion sprouted out from here, in Egypt?'

- Of course if they say it in the Bible, I allege.

- And do you know that Christianity acquired its mysticism in here?

- Are you Christian? I ask surprised.

- My grandmother was Copt; I am, I already have said it, mathematician. The religious tyranny has been the base of the human society from immemorial times. They have inserted an atrocious fear to the unknown, sowing in the human consciences 'yeast', amending all of the mass of ignorant people without mathematics.

'It has very curious results to observe the present society and see the amount of kicks the crowd points at them when they try to throw this wall, but the more they attack it, the most possibility they enjoy to survive, because they obtain strength from hate and from human despair.'

'They have created a force in society to desecrate the ones not haranguing as they do.'

'As religious forms do not develop at the same pace as human expansion, these outlines become shier each day, when presenting spirituality empty of human content.'

'Not only the Judaism and the Christianity have here, in Egypt, their origin and peak, but the two of them have committed the same error.'

'Moses placed the Arabs as enemies of the Jews. Being both of them children of Abraham, he invented a level for the true heirs, and left us as children of the enslaved woman.'

'To the Jews he called them to develop their spirituality and to us to worry for what is physical, although he was Egyptian, just as his woman.'

'But the same history demonstrates the opposite: the Jews are the ones not worried for the spiritual and they develop materially; and we, that supposedly were to act in a material way, we have being snatched out from the tangible development, and see each other fully up forced to a spiritual advance.'

'But I tell you something, whatever may be your origin and destiny, the only one representing truly the spiritual progress is Ishmael: 'I am against all, and all are against me'. There are no words more beautiful to catalog a searcher of the Truth.'

I found myself listening, still with my bathing suit on, an unusual and extremely beautiful explanation.

- Are the Jews not pleasing to you? I investigate.

- On the contrary, this one is the

reason why I returned from Sinai. I feel attracted towards the Jewish woman because she has a mental aggressiveness I admire. And because I fall in love very easily, to avoid problems, I returned to Cairo.

'In the beginnings of Christianity they dialogued at length and thought a lot on the nature of the teachings of Jesus. And they had several centers of associations. Jerusalem remained as a magnetic spiritual middle point, since it was there where Jesus was crucified.'

'Antioch was another core. Closely matched to Jerusalem and influenced, consequently, by Jews.'

'Istanbul was another one: there was the Caesar Court, and it attracted those who wanted to be in politics.'

'Rome remained with the commercial mentality of the roman people.'

'It was only here, in Alexandria. Have you ever being in Alexandria?'

- No, I answer.

- It was in Alexandria where the Christian ideas reach to the maximum. The greatest thinkers found in here an open and wide city for their principles.

'But again, the whole empire united and wasted Alexandria as the center of light. In the council of Nicea they deposed the heretics, the so called 'Gnostics', Arians, or knowledgeable of the spiritual reality, and extirpated from the western world the ones who did not accept the new dogma of the Emperor Constantine.'

'The fight between these two factions: the Arians and the Anti-Arians, although it is considered finished by many, continues alive in our human history.'

- Are you interested in what I am telling you? He argues suddenly.

- I am surprised of what you communicate me, I reveal; and I am, as they say, all ears.

- Jesus, for the Arians, is a man as we are, our brother, coming to us as Teacher to instruct us in our psychic development. He is, also, a great prophet for us, the Arabs.

'For the Gnostics he is with us constantly, integrated in all our human history, without giving up ever, very near us, not seated but working constantly in His task, that is common and unique for all humanity.'

'The 'Kingdom of Heaven' is not far from us, according to the Gnostics, but it is 'in' us. Jesus does not want any adoring people, but brothers working in His task, along with Him, helping all the human beings.'

'The Anti-Arians hold the opposite

position. Nowadays they call themselves Christians. But they have made their religion somewhat contrary to the original teachings.'

- You are lecturing me on religion, I assert, Are you sure you are not Christian?

- Of course not! this is precisely where I wish to go. All agreed to waste the Gnostics, Arabs in their majority, and again they relegate us, and still nowadays continues the same idea in all humanity. Now, as a result, thinking differently is ill, to reason and to investigate what is religious is forbidden. The only thing you are supposed to do is to accept what they tell you, they are wasting the intelligence.

'I am not follower of a group, because the entire association attempts a crime against your acuteness, they want to make you dolt, as they are'.

The young man speaks without raising his voice, with an astounding smoothness and without altering himself. I stay put seated in front of him, and I note the action of the massage, of opening new centers, continuing its functioning.

- So, not to lengthen me: they expelled all these heretics from here, some of them withdraw to the desert but the majority moved to northern Europe.

'Mathematically I find the human

history interesting and unpredictable, not even fiction is capable of foreseen the greatness of the human spirit.'

'In less of 100 years, these heretics' barbarians of Northern Europe, penetrated the South, destroyed the Roman Empire, and implanted their religion.'

'But was in Spain where the schisms produced a unique alchemy, therefore this is the reason I have to visit it. The Goth and Visigoth crossed the Pyrenees and Ataulfo self-proclaimed the first Spanish Goth king in the 410.'

'Gesalerico, in the year 507 self-proclaims the first Arian king.'

'In the 586 Recaredo bends down to the European pressure, abdicates his Arian faith, and becomes a faithful Roman Christian.'

'For more than 200 years, these Goth kings, they were originally the Arian Arabs, carried with them, from the steppes of Central Asia, the images of the Black Madonna's as emblems of their faith. They invited, once again, Arabs and Jews to join them in their universal cause, of starting a 'Human', 'Way', of 'Liberation'.

- You are giving me a class of history and developing new channels of information. I studied, when I was a child, those histories, but they bored me so much,

I never learned the names of those kings. Now you revealed them to me with surnames and dates.

- They translated, he continues, the sacred books and the Arian knowledge established a politic of perfect balance, no longer with two human groups, creating antagonisms, but with the harmony of the three: Arab, Christian and Jewish.

- What is that of the number three? I scratch. Can you explain it to me again?

- The number one, in mathematics, is God. The number two is the fight, the duality. The number three is the perfect balance.

'The harmony is not between two dissonant tones; it is found in the creation of a third pitch'.

'The most beautiful thing you have said to me tonight, without even noticing it, it is that I am 'the third Egyptian.'

'The people are confused, as are all those who decide to have enemies in order to survive. The balance is not in equaling the two weights, the scale represents a human being, 'the third', the one producing the union, the needed one, the desired, the indispensable.'

'The greatest secret I find in this world is not to discover who is your friend and who is your enemy, but on the contrary, what is the hidden force, private, secret, intimate, deep, integrating these two elements. The third unity, the one any of the two dares to reveal, because, if they manifest it, they both cease to exist as adversaries.'

'This is what I am trying to tell you: two human groups: Arab and Jewish, What is their center of attraction, the one neither of them has the courage to challenge? The answer is Egypt.'

'What is the hidden core, Christians or Arians disregard in dialogue, because if they discover it, both perish, attracted by it? The affirmation turns out again to be Egypt.'

'Search always, between friends and enemies, for that third person, or idea, the one nobody wants to be informed about because it is profoundly rooted in their beings, and gives the key for their mutual development and self-destruction.'

'When you discover the Third Dot, God reveals His essence to you, and so you do not any longer force anyone to accept your belief.'

'Toledo became, with the absence of Alexandria, the most luminous city on the planet.'

'All of it came to an end when Rodrigo (711), resigned during the Muslim invasion.'

'But we, with the incursion do not force conversion to the Islam, and so Gnosticism could develop by itself, implementing its own liturgy called 'Mozarabic'

'Jewish Gnostics established themselves in Gerona, and from there they gathered all their thought on the Kabbalah.'

'That Dark Age, as it is known in western history, was not dark at all for the universal thought or for the Arabs. The energy of learning merely exchanged its place of residence and from Toledo moved to Cordoba.'

'Our intelligent tendency of not representing the Divine in sculpture or painting, influenced greatly in the external austerity of the Arian ideas, and the thought concentrated in the study of the human body, of medicine and of the medicinal qualities of the plants.'

'With the arrival of the 'Catholic Kings', they had nothing 'catholic' or 'universal', the 31 of March of 1492, they expelled Arab and Jewish from the Iberian Peninsula, and a great period of darkness began, not only for Spain, but for the whole world.'

'The same year, the 12 of October, Christopher Columbus discovered a New World, and Christopher, which means 'carrier of Christ', moved the human development outside of Europe, creating new societies.'

'But, breaking up the number three, it all returns to the duality and crumbles'.

'Those holding power in Europe restarted the persecution against the "Spiritualists" or "Mystics", taking possession of the European thought, and forcing the migration of human beings, searching for unknown air for their spirits.'

'Millions of peoples were required to be baptized and accept a religion contrary to the original thought of Jesus.'

'Thousands of individuals, developing their spirituality by different paths, found in the new religion, more a submission to a European power, than a perfecting Way for their souls.'

"In all of it, we Arabs were immersed from the beginning, but we became invisible, as no one wants either to perceive or recognize.'

'We are the number Three, the one I told you, the hidden and dark force, the center of attraction, the one nobody dares to investigate. They even try to throw us from the human stream, refusing us as undesirable.'

'You can say you do not have any interest because you are not Arab, but I see the records of history as my own.'

'The Sphinx do not asks you in what you believe, but who you are. And when I observe the Sphinx, I perceive myself and I recognize me as human. She is the one who humanizes me, the number three, the perfect harmony, the secret center of the planet, taking care of the balance for all people.'

'She awaits, patiently, the confrontation and destruction of all the systems, and the rebirth of the human heart.'

- My father, I say, was a political prisoner, and he was shut in a concentration camp in Northern Africa, a flyer they clipped the wings. He helped me, in certain way, to understand a private history, rooted deeply in the hearts of men, contrary and opposed to the official history. Now it gives me reason for what you communicate.

'I am going to comment to you something very private, I tell him, since I came to Egypt I notice a presence of Jesus, so intense, as I never felt before.'

We remain in silence for a few seconds.

- When Plato visited Egypt, I continue, one of the priests spoke to him of Atlantis, and said some words that I always remember:

- You, Greeks, do think that you have

come very far away with the philosophy, but the Egyptian knowledge is far superior to yours, and you will not even attain the heels of our feet. But I want to add something else, he said, the cultures following you will be still lower, because humanity degrades with time.'

- I understand now, I continue, that your mathematical and human path is far closer to the thought of Jesus, than of those so called 'Christians'.

'I hold the opinion that all those of us who are incarnated, are the same people, reborn once and again until we attain our liberation.'

- There is a lot of population in the world longing for the times of Caesar, continues the masseur, in those years one person was the owner of the whole planet and he was surrounded by a pile of old people fighting among themselves to delight him. This evocation is a tendency gaining strength in the humiliation of the human being.

'And they go there, again and once more to acquire energy in their pompous ideas.'

'However, Egypt is precisely the opposite way of thinking.'

'They stole our obelisks, assessing the power of the intelligence that resides in them, but it is not so.'

The mathematics is part of our blood stream, and they could only be acquired if they join us. Relegating us, they obstruct themselves in their human development.'

'Those who base their own opinion on the more degrading tendencies of the human being, in their moral depth, in hate and enmity between the peoples, frighten humanity with its fear towards light and towards love.'

'And what for me it is a far more absurd, going against all mathematics and in opposition to any atom of intelligence, is that our present humanity has achieved to create a familiar religious form, taking you, from the day you are born until the day you die, leading you by the hand as if they were expert guides, without granting you any possibility of knowing other forms of thought or developing you in a universal way.'

'Our humanity is so absurd and so 'familiar', that each day we have more fences, so people remain paralyzed without any possibility either of going out or of entering.'

'The western way of thinking has come to this, when relegating the Arians and the Arabs; their form of thought becomes dead and can not be developed towards the future.'

'They have arrived at the lowliest in their degradation. From here it isn't going any farther. There is no longer anything else worse or to counteract the human development as the one who does not want to progress.'

'But, like the sun comes out for the good and bad alike, the sun will blunt it also for us.'

- It is curious what you are telling me, I express affirmatively. My father went from studying aviation in Russia, to a concentration camp in Africa. The barbaric Arians of Northern Europe unite again with his African companions. I never paid attention to this coincidence in the lifespan of my father. The Great Russian writers and musicians were for a long time my favorites. With your hands you have opened for me channels of human understanding, expressed marvelously.

- Which is your name? I ask him.

- Semsem, he responds.

- Has your name any meaning?

- Sem, in Arab, means sesame seed. Semsem is the diminutive; it can be translated as 'tiny sesame seed'.

- What a beautiful name, a seed so small, alive, healthy and pleasant. I am fascinated by sesame, and I always use 'gomasio' as salt.

- For us is a sign of tenderness, and indicates how small we are in relation to the universe, and how necessary it is to remain tiny in order to advance more, and to observe the minute details, those who explain excellently the wholeness of the idea.

- What you are telling me, I add, still is more beautiful.

- Your friend Joe, the one you spoke before of is correct, he confirms me. The entrance to the Pyramid has to be spaced out and buried: you must dig a lot, in the humbleness, to find the door.

- I am fascinated by sesame combined with honey, I fix, but when you refer to sesame, I remember the 'Open, sesame' of Ali Baba and the forty thieves.

- Do you know that this is an Arab fairy tale? He questions.

- Of course I know it, as are many stories and beautiful fairy tales.

- Do you know that 'Ali Baba' is an anagram of "Allah" and "Abba", of the God of the Arabs and the God of the Jews, than the Two are One? He awakens me with his asking.

- I did not know it, I communicate to him.

- Following the forty thieves through

the desert, Ali Baba, with the magic word of 'Open, Sesame', tore the small seed, and it burst in to the hidden cave in which are found great treasures.

'When you localize the number Three, you perceive the union between Allah and Abba, and in this connection is offered to you all the of the Earth's treasure.'

- Beloved Semsem, I enunciate, you are that seed opened for me. Your dialogue has surpassed the one from Plato. You have enlarged me with new paths of perception, and in your smallness have spread out in front of me the full cave of treasures of the Egyptian priests. What you have communicated tonight inundates my heart. I hope our Ways will cross again.

SECOND CANTICLE

UNEARTHING SPRINGS OF LIVING WATERS

THREE
SATISFYING WELLS

LOLA

When I published my book, I wanted to share it also with my friends of Algemesi, especially with 'Uncle Leonardo', a great sculptor and artist, whose spiritual vision always had attracted me. My home was next to his and my father modeled for him when he sculpted the monument to the music composer Cabanilles. Between my father and him, besides being relatives and neighbors, had developed a dearly friendship.

- Lola, I said to a friend, I am stopping at your house to give you a book I published, and after that, I will go to uncle's Leonardo house to leave him another one.

- Wait a little, answers Lola, better if you come to the Residence, and we will organize there a presentation for your book, I invite also Leonardo, and so we benefited each other by being together.

Twenty-one people assisted between theologians, priests, nuns, freethinkers and atheistic and pious people.

The meeting was alive and controversial.

Uncle Leonardo, during the reunion, wept of emotion for what he was catching.

Theo, in an abrupt intromission, where there is no one who can stop him, closed the presentation with his feeling, which opened like a box of light above all those attending.

When I returned a few months later, I went to say 'hi' to Lola and ask her opinion about the book.

Lola feels attracted for the Ecumenical Movement, that is to say: the union or understanding between the different religions, in which are integrated, not only the Christians, but also Muslims, Buddhists and Jewish.

Lola reads a lot and she works so that her view of mutual understanding may produce visible fruits.

During the past meeting she was radiant with light and joy seeing her ideals physically carried.

- Your book is lacking many things, she communicates me.

And this is why, possibly, she was expecting to read a book on spirituality, with pretty words and thoughts affirming her religious convictions, but it did not. The book produced in her an opposite reaction because it opened her frontiers. She had been so sure that it threw her into a spiritual anarchy, so difficult to understand by religious students.

- In relation to Manolo specially, continues Lola. It appears that he is your teacher and you only listen to him. You must write another book speaking of different people and ideas and overflow of Manolo's thought.

- You were my English language instructor, I tell her, and you know I was a bad student. My qualifications were low, and those only kept me afloat.

'I learned from the professors, studying from the outside towards the inside. They blunted my head with so many things, until the moment in which somebody stopped me.'

'It was a January 25 and Manuel Franco Rodriguez made me reflect on my life, and facilitated me to search within myself for the solution to all problems.'

'Then I began my work from the inside towards the outside.'

'It already happened before to Saint Paul, I continue, when after much study he fell to the ground, he throw away far from him the whole knowledge he had acquired in the school, and 'converted', he pierced beyond the mind.'

'The word 'conversion', where people think, consists in praying, in being good in front of others, and bending your head against any adverse circumstance of your life is the translation of the Greek word "metanoia".'

Now was Lola's turn to bear up my lessons.

- "Metanoia" it is composed of two words: "Meta", meaning "beyond". Metaphysical expresses "Beyond-physics", and "Noia", or "nus", denoting "mind". "Meta-Noia" connotes to go "beyond the mind". It searches for what is ahead of the thought, breaks through the mental wall and discovers a new world: the reality of the human feeling.'

'The mind, used to learn at the school, to reason and to instruct each other in different trades hardens with time, forming like a wall that hinders our access to other superior realities.'

'The mind, created to help us has altered into what Saint Theresa called 'the lunatic of the house', spoiling all of our existence.'

'When you "metanoia", transcend the mind, you find the world of the spirit, an intermediary zone where you perceive many spirits, incarnated or not.'

'Crossing beyond the environment of

the spirit you perceive the psychic territory, where evolution, free itself from the dominion of the mind extends until the Infinite.'

'John the Baptist preached the "metanoia" so people may transcend the mental area, and discovered the spiritual.'

'The Teacher came to give us the Baptism of Fire, so individuals could surpass the spirit to the world of the soul.'

'Therefore we cannot attain the Baptism of Fire without passing by the Baptism of Water.'

'Those who have written these sacred stories have done it to help us in our development. If you want to learn something you must discover a hidden world behind the appearances of the letters.'

'What you see in writing is annotated on the paper, but if you catch the spirit beyond the characters, you may perceive that, all of the venerable texts are infested with what I am speaking of.'

'But the humanity, instead of reading, analyzing them, and grasping their teachings, they are bounded to repeat the same traditions year after year, to 'convert' themselves, and returning to sin, and going back to reform, in a circle appearing increasingly to a hell of the one that cannot go out.'

'Without opening the manuals and without studying them, we have placed them on the altar and worship them as Sacred Books.'

'The Teacher is like a postman surrendering a message from God. Without opening it, we have placed it on the Altar to worship it, and on another Altar we have positioned him. And we kneel before Him, and ask Him things, and recount Him all of our problems, but we never open the letter.'

'Of Manolo, however, I continue, I never speak enough. There were not ideas what he taught, but feelings.'

'The thoughts can be changed, and truly we replace them constantly. All the religious forms have being imposed with schools and doctrines, engraved as in stone, with an implicit commandment that nobody can alter them; but in fact, however, all of them have being substituted and manipulated constantly.'

'The problem of the spiritual development is that there is too much knowledge, but not wisdom, excessive ideas, but without feeling.'

Lola goes out running and returns immediately loaded with six books:

- Look! She says, you must publish them in this way. Glance at this front page with a broken chain, which truly is a cover.

And you do not even want to read the book to understand the great message it carries. Have a quick look at this other...

I smile when I see so much worn-out money expend in texts, never well-read. And in her attack against the cover of mine, she illustrates that it was justly mine, the only examined manual. And I find myself happy when taking notice of my work reaching where the others could not.

- The teaching of Jesus, I continue, has not even a particle of knowledge. He shows only His feelings. He never lectures on the big theological themes that crush our religion. On the contrary, He displays in His parables feelings of the soul, activating in the listener, even today, after so many years, the desire of moving towards the heart.

'The ideas are unstable, modifying constantly; but the feelings are eternal, and their development does not involve destruction or annihilation, but growth.'

'The agreement in the spirit searched for in your meetings, cannot be forced, nor created with studies. The Unity of the soul already exists for the whole world. When we, human beings, cross the threshold of the spirit, we all perceive ourselves as a fraction of a same substance, which is Love. The only distinction between us, are the marks imprinted in our soul, on our terrestrial pilgrimage, by the many blows and ailments.'

- What do you want to tell me of your studies? She questions, opening a new chapter.

I begin to explain how I went to Merida, in Venezuela, worked as secretary of the Bishop and this one offered me the opportunity of returning to the seminary and graduate on my priestly studies.

- During the four years I stayed in the seminary of Caracas, I read all the Patristic, besides other books. I was a competent reader and a good student.

'The books of religion did not attract me in anything, but I went into the study of the Holy Scriptures. I got excellent marks and Bishop Perez offered me the possibility of studying in Rome and to obtain my doctorate in Bible... but some clerics oppose him. They wanted me to be a normal priest, a 'load mule', they said, working only on the base, without any possibility of climbing the stepladder of religious opulence.'

'As I was not interested in those kinds of honors, I declined the invitation, and accepted my assignment as 'priest of the people' in Mucuruba, and professor in La Salle in Merida.'

- And what about your priesthood? She insisted

- They anoint me priest 'according to the rite of Melchisedech', on the 25 of July.

'In agreement with Paul VI, under whose Papacy I was ordained, I am the only priest in the history of Catholicism 'being consecrated in the rite of Melchisedech'. This title is given by the Church, only to Jesus, with an honorary character.'

'My name appears in the Pastoral Letter, Archbishop Perez wrote on the occasion of my Ordination: 'The priesthood of the Church'.

'Paul VI even said to him:

- Be cautious with this young man, he is going to evaluate our Priesthood on Judgment Day.

'If Paul VI had said this 'Ex Cathedra...'

'The seminary of Caracas, when you graduate, offers a title equivalent to the Angelicum of Rome, under whose guardianship it shelters.'

'Outside of this one, I have no other parchment.'

'But 'eternal Priest according to the rite of Melchisedech', it is an epithet that no one possesses but me. I am the only one in the history of Christianity.'

'You have known me since I was a child, and have classified me in certain form. You never expected to read a book causing your inner self to be so upset, although it was not, nor it is, my intention.'

- And you do need to speak on prayer, she says immediately.

- Prayer, I answer, is not the repetitious mind submitting itself to someone else's guidelines. The authentic prayer is the work of our feelings, in constant dialogue with our conscience, with God.

'"Quid ora, labora" "The one praying is the one working", says the Christian doctrine. And it means that if you want to pray, you have to work. But it is not a physical labor, but the effort of creating feelings, bringing them out from our heart of stone.'

'My book, Lola, it is only prayer, a dialogue with my inmost God, trying to encourage those who search for Him in Truth.'

LORRAINE

With Sister Lorraine I conversed a few times. She was a Nun, a professor in India. She retired in South Florida after a life of education.

- Do you think we have known each other before? She asked me the first time I saw her.

- Yes, I expressed as answer.

- They call me Lorraine; she exposed spreading her delicate and firm hand.

- I invite you to breakfast and we will talk, she enumerated suddenly.

- You know, she began to explain once we were seated in the restaurant, I have spent all my life teaching in India. I lectured in all: from mathematics to religion.

'After retirement, I began to ask myself in what do I believe. Because I have taught a lot of devotion, but I realize that what I educated neither serves my pupils nor is it useful to me. Do you know the quantity of simplicity I imposed?'

'Now, in my old age, I have thrown far from me what I had in my mind, and have begun a new life based on the heart. What do you thing as an arrangement of existence when I am already with half a foot in the tomb?'

'When I lived in India I reflected a lot on reincarnation, and for me it made sense, but, these ideas were opposite to my formation as a nun and I could not speak of them with anybody. Now, already retired, I have begun to reflect on my own life and to feel what beats in my being.'

- Look! She whispered extracting a small paper in the form of a minute illustration, in which something is written.

I read it: 'one embrace has more value than one idea'.

The writing of the lithography spoke of the importance of the embrace, and finished the announcement with some words in capital letters:

'WE NEED FIVE HUNDRED A DAY TO KEEP EACH OTHER HEALTHY'

- You may keep it, in addition, she alleged, I am donating you some more in order that you may distribute them. Watch me now: an old nun promoting the embrace.

She finished her phrase with a smile of felicity, as of somebody who has found a key to penetrate in a new region.

- Nothing of which I taught had any value. Okay, she held, the mathematics is good to learn to count, but I am referring to the teaching of religion. I have lost my time explaining to others what unknown people wrote in books. And I remained, for all an existence, on a mental level, and the mind has not a technique to transcend to the heart.

'And so we are all nuns and priests. You know that the only things we teach are insipidities, and we spend our life, as strangers, without feelings, and after all of that we die. Whom are we going to find on the other side? We will be lonely forever, dead without feelings, destined to pray persistently but without producing any fruits. Therefore we need to embrace each other, to promote the contact of our spirits, and activate, with love, our hearts of stone.'

'Have you ever seen what we, nuns and priests, appear to be? We are seen as stone beings, with childish and immature ideas, pushing something in which nobody believes.'

'We are born human, as any other, but, as soon as they clothe us with the habit, we transform ourselves into tyrants.'

'When I retired, I hid my mantle in the closet, and I do not want to be buried with it, because I had to work hard to remove it.'

'The ancient Greeks spoke in their philosophy of "know thyself". At the entrance of each Greek temple could be read these words: 'Know yourself'.'

'Many years had past, but the great guides coming to our humanity, all of them have repeated these words, exchanging their wearing apparel and the accent:

'Jesus said:

'The true charity begins at home'

'Go to your house'

'You do not know yourselves and you do not know Me'

- Do you think, asked me Lorraine with a roguish smile, that the word "to know", in the biblical sense meaning 'to have sexual relation', has it some correlation with the "to know" of the Greek term?

'It says in the Bible that Adam 'knew' his woman and she begets a child; Abraham or Isaac or Jacob 'knew'. The biblical word gives an understanding that "to know" has some relation with another human being and of nakedness.'

- I do not think that the Greek word "to know" had the same meaning; I answered, trying to not incur in a dialogue about sex. The Greeks used other words. For example, they had had three words to qualify love:

'Philo' or the love you have with your family. The same word was used to designate tastes: I like oranges, or I love oranges. 'Philo-Sophia', translates as 'lover of wisdom' or 'Sophia'.

'Eros', is the 'erotic love', or the carnal or flesh relations.

'Agape', or 'unselfish love', translated as 'charity'.

- It is my opinion that the Greeks used the word "to know" like a form to pierce the mind and reach, not knowledge, but wisdom.

'This "know thyself", is an inside search, I continued saying.'

'The Teacher said many times that the 'Kingdom of Heaven' is in us. When they say to each other there is in here or in there, do not pay attention, because the 'Kingdom of Heaven' is found in us. It is near, within our hand's reach, in our heart.'

'The parables of Jesus, do not refer to 'soup opera stories', but to personal psychic situations, private for each human being, and at the same time common, since they belong to all the humanity.'

'The 'Kingdom of Heaven', looks like the owner of the house that, from his chest, brings out, observes, analyzes and turns back to hide what he finds, the new and the old experiences. This refers to everyone of us, when we are owners of our own actions, we must, to find the 'Kingdom of Heaven' in us, extract with our feelings, the memory of past personal experiences, and investigate them, scrutinize them, watch them with the eyes of our heart.'

'We discover in our existentialist stories, germinal dreams of our own Ego, guiding us to the future. We evaluate the past from the future, and discover it without broadcasting any judgment, but feelings of love. And we return them to our chest, to keep them where they were; we have to move them, hidden and secret, into our belongings trunk.'

'The ten virgins, I continued saying, waiting for their husband, are our senses. In agreement with the human knowledge, we have five senses. At present we are conscious of having some more, and many more sprout in us as we advance. But, the Teacher uses the five: seeing, hearing, tasting, touching, smelling, and folds them into ten, since five are 'stupid', because they only relate to the physical, and five are 'sensible', related, besides the tangible, to the spiritual.'

'The ten senses fall asleep, because we do not use them. We do exercise either the physical or the psychic ones'.

'When the 'husband' arrives the five

cherished senses are prepared to weigh anchor to the intimate encounter and the five 'dimmed', without 'oil', the carnal or fleshy ones, have to go out to buy it, since it cannot be manufactured. To these, the husband does not 'know' and cast them to the darkness of the outside world.'

'If you analyze each Parable, I continued, you will understand that each one of them refers to you, it is only for you, in order that you may develop, and could open your senses for this mystic union with your inner self.'

'You discover, then, your smelling, tasting, seeing, touching and hearing being sleep, atrophied in the irresponsibility of the society in which you live.'

'God has created for you a wonderful and grandiose world, with plenty of fruits and vegetables, with a smell that might distinguish a hue thousands of diversities and you limit yourself to your 'favorite perfume'. From the thousands of fruits and vegetables you fence yourself only with the taste of the apples and cucumbers. Instead of enjoying each terrestrial landscape, you are attracted only to the place where you were born or where you vacation. You refuse to develop your touch to feel God, hiding your hands in the pocket, and do not even touch with your fingers whatever enters into your mouth. Without listening to the music broadcasting in each human heart, each animal, each plant, each leaf of the forest, you blunt your ears with the strident noise that society imposes.'

- You are expanding me, fixed Lorraine stopping my speech, into the necessity of embracing, touching, smelling each other.

- Do you realize that we are the ones who have eyes and do not see, ears and do not listen, mouth and do not speak, hands and do not touch, noses and do not smell?, I continued.

'The spirituality is a self-discovery.'

'The Parable of the ten virgins is not to be examined from the outside, but to be explored, to 'know thyself', awakening your senses, so these may unite with your spiritual Ego, producing "oil", feelings of love, giving you the materials so you could set on fire your light, when your husband, your spirit, appears.'

- Now you are talking as a nun, Lorraine stopped me, because the majority of us, nuns, offered each other to Jesus as our spouse. Have you ever asked yourself if He wants to marry us? Is He attracted to wed with a piece of stone, a woman only desiring to caress Him externally, prevaricating to lose herself, throwing the

Ego into a channel with a Love that wastes and redeems you? Has Jesus such a bad taste, as to select that heap of lonely? Or do we believe Him so simple, and without own will, as to fulfill all of our toxic desires of a Redemption without Love?

Lorraine executed her series of questions with a malicious and roguish smile. Never had I found a nun, or in other words, a being, as herself.

Lorraine was the first one telling me of the DNA of the soul.

- We have come many times here to earth, she specified. Each one of our existences is like a thread in a great tapestry.

'We think many times that our history mixes all of it, as if it was an amorphous soup. But every one of our entities is completely different.'

'The colors absorbing our eyes, the fragrance our smell remembers, the tone of each human voice, the material chemical quality of the souls surrounding us, the experience of every one of our cells, being part of us, and we do not even know they exist; each particle of the whole is unique, without deformity, lacking blend, perfectly pure.'

'Each one of them experiences contacts or unions with other millions of cells, but, with no mixing, devoid of broths, without losing their individuality, their purity, their virginity.'

'The history of our souls is so enormously great and sublime, that if many books were written, they could not contain the wealth of information so huge, that every one of them contains.'

'Therefore each existence is like a thread, immaculate, pure, certain, and when observing its string on the tapestry of your being, your soul begins to acquire that weight.'

'Then you observe a new world, without sexual characteristics or basic distinction among human beings. You discover Love. And as we have gone out of Love, and to Love we return, Love eliminates all barriers of race, sex or social order.'

'Our soul has an eternal DNA and each cell holds memory of each friction it had since its remote creation, and will possess it for all eternity.'

A few months later, they offered Lorraine work with the sick AIDS patients in St. Leo College. She sold the little property she had, and resided in the College, living together with the religious priests.

- Sometimes I feel tired and I do not know if I have an impact with the students or not, if I help them to search for their own selves. Now in my old age, it helps me to discover more love and to promote my five hundred daily hugs. I have turned out to be like Mary Magdalene: in love with Jesus and surrounded by men, priests, watching me suspiciously; she told me, flashing her roguish smile.

- Since the first word you pronounced, when reading the Gospel, I knew we had to know each other and share our feelings. Do you think we have known each other before? She insisted

When questioning me, she photographed in the ether the answer, and then I saw her, as a maid, in Jerusalem, in the times of Jesus.

- Yes, I told her, we have known each other in many lives. I cannot display for you the roads you have crossed, but I know that wherever you have gone, you carried out your light. Our encounter is short, but how happy am I sharing our essence.

A few months later Lorraine moved to the other side. I attended her funeral in the College Chapel. It was packed with young students, wanting to say goodbye, thanking her for what she did for them. The temple was crammed and I had to remain at the door, weeping constantly when verifying with how many hundreds of students, she shared her light.

A clamor of sparrows blasted her transit with their canticles.

The priests of the College dedicated to her the building of their residence, across from the Chapel.

Lorraine is a being that knows herself, she is aware of the strength of Love and with her five hundred daily embraces she caressed many human hearts.

VILMA

- Look what I have written! Vilma says as soon as I enter her home.

Vilma likes to read, and she is a beloved friend.

She offers me some thirteen leaves of paper.

- This is what I think on Christianity. Here are some of my prayers; what I have been writing for some time; it is my guideline.

The front page contains what for Vilma is the essence of her faith:

'From the Gospel of Thomas:

Jesus said to his Apostles:

- If you extract what is in you, whatever you bring out will save you: When you find it, it will disturb you and what will disturb you will amaze you.

- When you achieve to know yourself you will be rich.

- But if you do not know yourselves, then, you will die in your poverty and you are that poverty.'

- Vilma, I tell her, you always liked these ideas.

- Yes, she informs me, since I read the Gospel of Thomas and analyzed these beautiful words; I have taken them as guide of my life.

- 'If you extract what is in you, what you bring out will save you' she continues. Have you brought out what is in you?

- Precisely, I answer, we have always conversed on those things.

- 'When you find it, it will disturb you'. Has that occurred to you? She inquisitively continues.

- Yes, I answer, this disturbance, disconcert or embarrassment, you carry it for your whole life. The history of our human existences, when we discover them, it is amazingly interesting and they cause us perplexity.

'They look like, I continue, as a pendulum that it goes from side to side. First you go towards the extreme right, later on you move to the farthest left, afterwards, again to the utmost right, and so on constantly, and sometimes, the change occurs even in this same lifetime.'

'Those who cross over conservatives spring up modern, those who die 'in the latest fashion', return in rags. Therefore, when you find these oppositions in your personality, you are stunned and lead astray.'

'For example, in reference to the reincarnation, people imagine the following: I like luxury, and powerful men, the wealth and Egypt, therefore I believe I have been Cleopatra in a previous life.'

'And it is precisely the opposite. When Cleopatra reincarnates, she does not want to know anything of Egypt, or of Marc Anthony, or of power or riches, but chooses a remote part of the planet, contrary to Egypt, and she is born as Maori in New Zealand.'

'That is why you are disturbed, because you could never imagine what you were before. Furthermore, today you hate what you did in the past. Love what today you despise and it will lead you to what you were previously.'

'Continue your saying: 'what disturbs you will amaze you', and truly, these words are from Jesus, or from someone that has discovered his essence.'

- Why aren't these things expressed publicly, and the apocryphal gospels relegated to the absentmindedness, when really they can help us to a better understanding of Christianity and to get out of absurd beliefs that have very little to do with Jesus?

- The message brought by the Teacher, I explain, is an announcement of personal development, private and concealed. Constantly He repeats in the Gospel that this process of psychic growth has to remain hidden.'

'When you pray to your Father do it hermetically, may nobody notice it, and your Father, who sees what is secret, will answer you.'

'When you give alms, may your right hand know not what your left is doing.'

'When you fast, may nobody perceive it, if not, you have received your reward.'

'Clean out yourself, exhale your perfume, smile, may nobody grasp it.'

- It also says, confronts Vilma, 'what I tell you in secret, proclaim it from the rooftop'

- It means, I reveal, 'what I inform you in your inner self announce it from your conscience'. The Christian road is a personal advance transpiring in the unknown of the soul.'

'The word 'secret', naturally, has been despised by all humanity, and so we have been told that 'to hide' something is bad; we need to publish it all, so the whole world will identify it; we must waste the 'secret societies', as somewhat dreadful and necessary to extirpate from the people.'

- Then, continues Vilma, are you saying that what is in us cannot be published and proclaimed to the crowd?

- The word 'secret', has a different meaning for Jesus, I continue. For Him it denotes 'spirit'. And so, we could understand the previous phrases of Jesus as: 'When you pray, plead in the spirit...', 'When you give alms, provide them in the spirit...', 'When you fast, refuse to eat in the spirit...'

'And, to answer your question: 'What I tell you in the spirit, proclaim it from the rooftop, express it in your conscience.'

'The process, the teachings, the work, the occupation of the human being must be developed spiritually, so this process would not be understood by the flesh, by the human mind.'

'For the human understanding, all this practice remains veiled, and cannot be reasoned, or deciphered.

'But just imagine something else. Once they asked the Teacher to instruct them in the spiritual world and He said:

- If I tell you of material things and you do not learn, how are you to be tutored in psychic organisms?

'We are beings working in two realities: the material and the psychic. The work is in the two levels. But we are One, and we cannot wear away this Unity. Therefore when we forge something, small as it may be, it has repercussions not only on the physical, but also in the moral.'

'The duty must be performed here, in what is solid, with our mental tool, but guessing that our labor is not only coarse, rough or clumsy, but psychic, sensitive, delicate. The absolute director must be our soul, not our mind.'

'Therefore, when the followers of the Way, that was the first name given to the disciples of the Teacher, began to extend for the planet, they did not have temples, or liturgical laws, or gods... they were completely different from the rest of the peoples.'

- Look at the comments in this book, says Vilma, rising from her seat to search for an obese volume of history.

- A Roman historian, Celsus, in the II Century, wrote a book making fun of Christians: because they did not possess temples, or gave offerings to the gods, nor did they have any altars. He ridiculed them saying that while the rest of the world's people maintain many gods, the Christians were so poor they had only one.

'He also criticized them because, according to Celsus, we all know that when we die everything finishes and we move to 'the naught'; those who follow the teachings of Jesus think that life does not end, but that we rise again, and they accept reincarnation as true.'

'Celsus completed his work pronouncing that Christians had no religion, and therefore it could not be approved by Caesar.'

'Origen, continues Vilma reading over the top, a Father of the Church, answered him with another book entitled: 'Against Celsus', in which he defended the Christian viewpoint, in which they had lived for more than two hundred years.'

- But Vilma! I attempt to stop her and return to the original conversation.

- The Roman emperor Constantine, she continues reading, had not been a Christian, gathered all representatives of the Church in the Council of Nicea and told them he was already tired of arguing with so many faithful, demanding from them to create a religion, with temples, altars and gods, and Jesus would be proclaimed 'God', as was the Caesar.

'What is this book uttering? She questions insistently. Was it Jesus, before Emperor Constantine would approve it, not God? Is this the truth?'

- Some historians, I clarify, hold the opinion that Emperor Constantine asked

Pope Sylvester to be killed on the 31 of December. While he distributed the consecrated bread during the Mass, a murderer approached him, received communion, and immediately stabbed him. It was not only the end of a year, but the cease of the original Way.

'The Roman noblemen donated their houses and transformed them into Temples... and we moved to another page in history.'

- But, insists Vilma, answer to my question of what this book is tackling: Is it true that Jesus, in the primitive faith, was not God?

- Vilma, I cannot answer your inquiry. You are stirring at the central point of what is precisely the essence of our conversation.

'You have begun to meditate on your faith, continue going deeper into it, and bring out from you the whole knowledge kept in your heart for eternities.'

'But, and here I am answering your question: do not ask me, neither anybody to give you a reason to have faith, because the Teacher constantly asks the same question to all his followers:

- Who do you think that I am?

'Moreover, I continue, He does not want anybody to tell the neighbor that He is the Messiah. Each one of us has to search for Him by our own account.'

'And we all, dear Vilma, we load in our individual being the answer, private and veiled, to your question.'

'This is what you must bring out from you, the spiritual answer reaffirming you. When you find it, it will disturb and amaze you. When you achieve to observe yourself you will be rich. But if you refuse self-knowledge, and search for approval in external books or documents, then you will die in your poverty and yourself, when you refuse your inner self, you will be that poverty.'

THIRD CANTICLE

COMING ACROSS SECRET SHELTERS

THREE SANCTUARIES

MADELYN AND DEL

Del and Madelyn are two good friends. He is an excellent tennis player. She is a very good, 'Cicliptic Planetologer', as she designates herself.

- Not only you, dear friends, but a lot of people ask me if I believe in reincarnation, I remark to them.

'I do not like at all, personally, the word 'believe', as it designates to accept what others tell you. I am fond of the English word "believe" because in the center of the word is localized 'lie'. What means to say: the one declaring 'I believe', is lying,'

'We all are full of opinions leading us by confused paths. What is a supposition does not pilot you to anything, or to a change of conduct, because all of your affirmations disappear like the smoke, when somebody else presents to you a different view.'

'To believe' has not directed anyone to the 'metanoia': to move beyond the mind, but on the contrary it plunges them in a lethargy of the one that cannot come out, and of the one that has been qualified as 'opium of the people'. Since the countries retaining many beliefs doze in an infernal past of the one which can not be freed.'

'To have 'Faith' is somewhat completely opposed. The certainty is what moves the mountains of the mind, the one forging new humanities and creating civilizations of light. The security is obtained when you transcend the mind, and know tiny fragments of the Only Truth.'

'The Faith is attained with work, study, metanoia, stepping up to the spiritual level and, still as a human being, and without moving from the place where you are located, you pronounce these words that wrap of light your spirit: 'I know.'

- In the Age of Aquarius, cuts Madelyn, the time in which we are entering now, we all will be capable of pronouncing these words. In the Era of Pisces, the one we are leaving, we all announced 'I believe'.

- Would that, I continue, answering your question, I do not believe in reincarnation, but I know of it, because I have seen myself in different personifications.

'We indulge in our humanity millions of people believing in reincarnation and other hundreds of groups not accepting it.

But both fractions are equal, because all of them are motivated by their beliefs, and the society remains static.'

'It has been already more than twenty years, when seated in my office, someone called at the door.

- Come in! I say.

- May I? Questions a young woman opening timidly the entrance, not knowing who was inside.

- Of course you may! Approach ahead! Sit down! I say offering a chair.

- They call me Irma, indicates the young woman introducing herself. I was praying in there, in front of the statue of the Virgin, and she asked me to recount to you what I saw.

I thought on other pious revelation, where they attack your freedom, asking you for hours and hours of prayers, with the only aim of boring you and wasting your life.'

- So, tell me what you want; I remark exposed and resigned not offend her.

- It is fine! I do not know where to begin, she answers.

'I gave a sign indicating to her that I was prepared to listen. But for more than five minutes she was searching for words. Five minutes, as below water, for the tension and the waiting.'

- Do you believe in reincarnation? She questions, wanting to investigate into my beliefs.

- Yes, I specify as answer.

'When we read the Bible, without preconceived thoughts, with no information about Abraham, Moses, Jesus; what is to say, like a normal book of the one you do not know what it's all about; if we scrutinize so the Bible, we will discover many references to reincarnation.'

'What bounce most in the Gospel is Jesus revealing several times that the spirit of Elijah reincarnates in John the Baptist.'

'With Nicodemus He had a conversation about been 'born again', which it is a translation of the word "reincarnation".'

'Jesus also asks His listeners:

- Who do people say that I am?

- A few say Elijah, Jeremiah, or one of the prophets, answer his disciples returning to ancestral beliefs.

- And, knowing me better, who do you say that I am? Ask them Jesus in return.

- You are the Messiah, the Son of God, answers Peter.

'Which we may translate as: You are the Messiah. You have prepared yourself for a long time, but, in this human generation, you have only been incarnated now, this is your only and exclusive incarnation. You come directly from God.'

'On a different occasion, conversing over the blind man from birth, to better understand the mechanisms of reincarnation, the disciples ask Jesus:

- Who sinned, this one or his parents, in order that he would be born blind?

- Neither this one, nor his parents, answered Jesus; but in order for us to heal him.

'And that is, as always, another authoritative answer: the problems are not to be broadcast, but to be solved,'

'To whom does it matters the scrutiny of the why of the blindness, if we do not reach to the effectiveness of the solution?'

'To me, personally, I still find in a Psalm, my affirmation on reincarnation:

'To Jerusalem we call mother,
Because we all have been born in it.
In the register of each human being
We find in writing:
'This one already was born there'
And they will sing, while dancing:
'All my sources are in you'

'To say-so that in my personal registry there is a note revealing 'This one already was born there', leaves me openmouthed. Because, it brings to light, that we all have to be incarnated there.'

'The Teacher, coming only once, also was born there.'

'And to say-so 'all my sources are in you' means that whatever better happened in every one of our lives has been to be born in Israel.'

'Since this passage opened my understanding, I hold it as a base for the study of the Bible. In it I see the development and evolution of our humanity, not of the Jewish people, but of all our generation, in our passing through Jerusalem.'

'The prophets, judges, inhabitants all of Israel are the souls of all the peoples: Asians, Arabs, Europeans, Africans, Americans, Polynesians, Australians: all we have been born there. The Bible reports the history of all our evolution, in our transitory path through Jerusalem.'

'The prophets are souls of diverse places of this Earth, and each of them contributes his own discovery to the only human channel of redemption.'

- Salvation comes from the Jews, says Jesus.

'And we do not understand Him because we think that are the Jews those giving us salvation, but Jesus answer is a conflicting one: salvation comes from the Jewish flow because we all have been born there, as we all are in the same stream, only one watercourse unique and well arranged.'

'Jerusalem translates as 'City of Peace', a metropolis that has killed all its prophets, a municipality belonging to all the human races.'

"Wish Peace to Jerusalem": this has been the indication of the great prophets: promote in your heart an energy of Peace on Jerusalem in order that the religions would disappear and the human spirit may be united, with Peace, to share each human experience, being every one distinctive, diverse and at the same time common and beneficial for us all.'

'An intimate practice, with only one flock and one shepherd, untied of religions that divided the indivisible current of the spirit.'

'But I only answered 'Yes' to Irma, wishing not to explain details of my biblical investigation.'

- It is fine! She starts the speech slowly, preparing an unknown terrain for her. The Virgin told me to tell you that She loves you dearly... that She always has cared for you... that when the Messiah incarnated... you knew Him...

'Irma spoke with intermittent phrases, blushing with each word, and with sporadic spaces. She presented me something completely new, a bit that my brain saved in its memories.'

'She spoke to me of my different incarnations. For me all of it was beautiful in a 'soap opera' style. But when I asked her for names or dates, she refused to give them to me.'

- I cannot communicate them to you, she insisted.

'So I remained a little perplexed trying to conjecture and scrutinize suppositions. I am bored with the attempt, leaving me bothered and so, I cornered it to the side.'

'Ten years later, I visit Antonia, a woman, a healer with the impositions of hands, and that one morning she appeared all covered with biblical characters; facts that fascinated even the Holland press. They took many pictures of her and she answered:

- I have lived in the Bible

- Bring me a tape, because I am going to record on it what you have been in other lives, she says as soon as I sit at her side.

'And Antonia recorded a cassette tape of what she went saying.'

'When I asked her about some issues, differing a little from Irma's communication, Antonia always stopped me saying:

- Not! That is not so!

'And she described all of it as Irma referred it to me ten years before in a different continent.'

'I located her revelation at the side of the other one unintentionally analyzing it or studying it. Because they were somewhat unconnected with me, and I did not know how to accept them.'

'Some time later, talking with Manolo about reincarnation, I exposed him the two revelations, those of Irma and Antonia.'

- Throw them out of your mind, he tells me, because they cause you pain.'

'And I eradicate them from my conscious brain moving them to the luggage trunk of recycling.'

'A few years ago, being in front of the Samurais door, in the Imperial Palace of Tokyo, suddenly I saw myself in another existence, as Japanese.'

'And in there, along with all the display of a previous life, I understood the teaching of Manolo.'

'And it is this one: when your study the reincarnation, you do analyze with your mind what others offer you, but all of it are alien and external ideas, where they describe your past lives as if out a novel, recounted from the exterior, as it was done to me by Irma and Antonia.'

'When you see who you had been,

what first springs up in your mind is a rejection against the professor that instructed you erroneously.'

'I, from the Samurais' door shouted back to my previous coach:

- Stupid! How wrongly you have educated me insinuating that the Japanese are superior to the Chinese! Useless person! I holler him from the future to a past becoming present: when you know that the Chinese are excellent.

'I perceived the instructor informing me from the outside towards the inside. My ancient guide was similar to Irma and Antonia: they were describing my clothing, my past covers.'

'And when the vision of the past turns present and you see how wrong you behaved always, dressed with beautiful wearing apparels, but without soul.'

- Are your Elijah? They ask John the Baptist.

- Not! He answers.

'In his reply there is a great teaching, because we always refuse what we were in a previous life.'

I continue the account of some past conversations.

'Ricardo is a youth remembering his previous life. I knew him when his father invited me for dinner at their home. During the supper he stayed concealed without saying word. The conversation was animated, speaking on religion and studies.'

- Atheism is taught in the Catholic schools, Ricardo said in his only intervention, inducing all of those present to turn their heads, surprised, when listening to an assertion so firm.

'After supper I comment him on Elijah, and he replies:

- When you cross over and perceive how much you have deviated from your goal, your past produces such a huge repulsion, you do not want even to remember it; you refuse it with all your energy, as it leads you to failure.

- And family ties, I ask, do they take us beyond reincarnation?

- They do not! He answers me with authority, because all of it is deceit. The only persisting factor is the assignment of each human being. All the encounters occurring in our life are related with our task; I do not want to know either my past mother or my previous brothers.

'The family unions are for this life. But if these relatives' ties are not rooted in your task, they will disappear as soon as you cross over.'

'The different levels of evolution of the human being must be crossed alone, continues Ricardo. If you are not qualified, you cannot enter.'

- In reference to the physical forms, I ask him, do they maneuver towards a human ideal of perfection and beauty?

- On the contrary, he explains, you acquire the form you want, with its qualities and defects, in agreement with the assignment you have, to carry out a better labor. But what is flesh remains decaying; the spirit, flourishes immortal.

'The race has very little to do with the psychic substance. And always there is a key of union to complete between an existence and the other, he affirms.

- We reincarnated to acquire more knowledge, promulgates Madelyn.

- Not! I indicate. What is important is not the knowledge, but to find the Door. Many times what we learn slows down our advance and delays our incentive.

'We come to this world, once and again, to fulfill our duty, but as we do not carry it out, we reappear again trying to do it.'

'The Teacher came here only once, to redeem us all, and He had enough with three years and a half; He created and builds now a quantity of masterpieces, of whose, a tiny amount are in writing; catch sight of His great and important task. We, having nothing to manufacture, compared with His', we gather once and again, lengthening each other in our eternal task.'

'What they have described to me is only the dress I already had. They cannot disclose my soul, because only I may reveal it.'

'The teaching of Manolo is certain: only tossing from my mind what others had given me, it caused my spirit to activate on the way to find his own essence.'

'I have seen some of my previous lives, and what Irma and Antonia said, was partially fulfilled. But they, on revealing my past, showed me only the wearing apparel.'

'When I detected what was hidden, I discovered my intimacy, and this one turned me over criticizing the ones guessing me what is the opposite; because they only showed me the appearances, the disguise, what is external, the form of my mind; but could not reveal me the Truth, neither the essence, or the inside, nor the work of my spirit.'

'We drag all of it, from incarnation to incarnation, as handicaps, until we open this magic Door and discover our soul'.

'Then all these pedant mistakes, when reflecting the light of the spirit, it turns luminous, and our incapacities acquire irradiation.'

'In my case I could observe the Zen Philosophy glued to my soul; it accompanies me for my lifespan, being a dear part of my being: the desire for minimal things, the simplicity of life, the order and the cleaning of the ideas and in the daily work, the taste for a naked dip, the pleasure of the hot springs, the water as religion, the true baptism of John.'

'I have returned to Japan again, and each time I am happier with my handicap.'

- Have you written something lately? Interrupts Madelyn, Why do not publish these observations in a book?

- Now that you are asking me, I answer, I did e-mail these to a friend and maybe, it may turn into a book. I extract a piece of paper from the folder and I read aloud:

"Yesterday I went, with Theo, for a stroll through the temples of Kyoto. A young Japanese approached and asked us:

- May I take your picture?

I assented nodding and he took our picture.

- May I take yours? I asked him in return.

- Of course, he answered my question, with all my love.

He opened his chest and modeled for us.

I am recounting you these deeds and you may think I am inventing them. But this is a reality we experience daily, not only me, but every human being. From where do we know each other? Why this interest in taking my picture? Which way has traveled his soul? What trail trek has this one human being taken in order that he crossed with mine?

We can not even communicate each other with the language, and our paths split again, but that second of union, without even touching him, produces a sparkle in the soul, which transports me to the Infinite, and to an intangible reality, alive, luminous and loving.

We did intersect by places and find beings we loved, and evoked them with affection. If we did suffer, or they were our enemies, we inspect them with resentment, guessing again the attack.

I have been drawn out of many places; in others I was received as a dearly loved one. I study what transpires around me. I hunch an intuition I did wrong with many people; to others I love them madly and know we all are integrated in the same undertaking.

So, do not accept reincarnation as a belief. Waste it far from you, and start analyzing the tiny details of your life: the bonsai you have at home, the first time you tried sushi, the thousands of daily experiences; and in them you will perceive what they are giving you: the key of access to your soul.

And when those moving collections from Ancient Persia, Egypt, Mexico, China, Cambodia, Hawaii, Thailand... or modern artists showing their skills arrive at your city, you will perceive them, dear friend, revealing to you, your own being, and they will offer it to you in order that, from it, you will seize only love, architect of each object, and through it, you may achieve to connect with the soul of the artist.

But you will discover it with disgust. First, because you do not want to go. Second, since you are not attracted. Third, because inasmuch as they push you against your will towards a culture of any interest to you. And if through any object of art you may look inwardly, to your internal being, then it will open for you the Doors of Paradise.

You will discover having been in many places, you will find out we all human beings are 'One spirit', and you won't classify anyone as alien, not even as brother, because all of them are you and each human fraction is a part of your only breath.

The clothing differentiates us,

imposing borders to our essence.

When guessing the nakedness of conscience you will discover a single humanity without boundaries.

You won't be the Pharaoh, Emperor, Cleopatra or Plato. Your inside perception will be open and you will distinguish yourself, at their side, and you will know your soul and your essence.

You will perceive our earliest instructor, still stupid, promoting animosity, this time no longer as Japanese, but as a North American trying to relegate the Japanese.

The ancient Emperor is still sleeping endlessly, unintentionally wanting his world of power and terrestrial brilliance stumps in forgetfulness... How difficult it is for the rich people to enter the Kingdom of Heaven.

You will find out your ancient companion, still at your side.

I have seen our former chief of Samurais, to the one we informed, working as a chemist in Poland, despised by his own family. He is already entering through the narrow door; but his wife and children continue with their desire of political power and the wealth that perishes.

Our ancient enemies are still charging around and exhausting us.

But, little by little, when one of them crosses to the Light, gives up all his clothing of hate, and the suit of being naked transforms him in 'One' and already he is a fraction of us.

- We lament ourselves, I say leaving the paper and reflecting, of the wrong we behaved towards each other, and this gives us an attitude of sincere humbleness, without pretense.

- In my studies, says Madelyn, I could verify that all over the whole planet they study reincarnation, but we, Christians, are afraid to analyze it, thinking these opinions will ravage our faith; when it is completely quite contrary: our faith increases when we know God as 'Just' and repaying us according to our actions.

'I have produced some studies, naming them 'Cicliptic Planetology', it is a knowledge of the soul, mind and body and its integrated development with the planets, not the stars.

'Do you know that the universe is crammed with galaxies and worlds of those whom we cannot even imagine?'

'The reincarnation is the only correct theory, since it is a sure thing, the progress of the human being, and, without everlasting life, all our being will finish in the tomb and in the naught.'

'Once I had a vision of the Teacher in which He said to me:

- How much would I want them to take me out of the cross, because I am the Resurrection.

'It was like if He was telling me: I am the One giving you the energy to come back to life again.'

DON JOSE

- Do you know, asks Don Jose, the tourist guide of Cusco, during the farewell meal, that we, the Quechuas, cling to the traditions given to us by our ancestors, because these believes are more powerful than the ones furnished to us by the Spaniards? We have made a special union between the two of them, giving us security in our steps.

- This is extremely interesting, I ratify, because when coming here I was certain I would find a lost brother, and had a presentiment of him been half Quechua and half Christian, but until the present, I have not come across him.

- During our history, many have achieved to penetrate in the world of the spirits, finding the split of division between these two places.

'Very little of what they discovered comes to light and, besides, the tiny becomes mythology. Many tourists make fun of it and criticize it as being part of the folklore of a poor people. Therefore our knowledge is silenced more privately than before.'

'My ancestors divided the world into three parts, superposing them in the shape of a Cross, based astronomically in the Cross of the South, as the central mark of their celestial reference:

- The Condor rules the spiritual element.

- The central plane, or the mental, it is represented by the Puma.

- The Snake indicates the world of the dead.

'Each one of these spaces is perfectly edged; it has its own laws. The man, in his walking, moves among them, and he has to respect the norms in agreement with the level in which he finds himself.'

'These three parts are all included and integrated in the human being; they respect each other among themselves. The Condor, in its majestic flight represents God; the violent Puma, the human way of doing things; the Snake is not the symbol of what is wrong, but the wisdom leading us with certainty through the world of the spirits.'

- I especially appreciate what you have shown me during these days, dear Jose. When you told me that Jesus was your Teacher, you left me perplexed, because I could not comprehend where you were coming from, but when you communicated to me your vision and His words, I could understand all of it.

'Do not waste your body with sugar', I empathized immediately with you, because your Teacher was my Teacher. And I could say that I got out of Peru, without finding my brother, but with my faith embedded, not in a small stone, but in Waina Pichu. So it is our Teacher: strong, healthy, extremely beautiful and magnetic.

- The Way of each human being is different and unique, continues Jose. What one discovers, in proportion with the social opposition, remains very limited to a reduced circle of people.

'The knack of union with the spiritual has been unlocked from the beginning of human creation. The Patriarchs and the entire Biblical people were clairvoyant, revealing the world of the spirit, and they tried to channel their followers towards it. Their experiences lasted in familiar and tight circles.'

'Not only them, but also us and the Hindus, the many African tribes, the Polynesians, Japanese, Spanish... all humanity has had clairvoyants, or as you want to call them, as originators of their spirituality.'

'People, who do not posses inside vision, materialize it, creating religions.'

'But even nowadays, if we get immersed in a spiritual development, the society forces us to keep ourselves in secret or private meetings, not to hover something bad, but by public rejection of those who do not understand, criticize and despise us.

'Even the Teacher, a exceptional human being endowed with psychic qualities, more than we can imagine, explained all of this 'privately' to his disciples and revealed to them the essence of His parables.'

'But I find, continues Don Jose, in the letters of Paul, an explanation of what happened in our culture before the coming of the Spaniards. In the meetings of our ancestors, and even today, when we get together with other Quechua groups there is a presence of spirits communicating with the living.'

'I see the material world and the globe of souls, as two spheres demanding to inter-penetrate each other, but they repel, since the spiritual collides against what is material.'

'But when you discover the point of union between these two spaces, then all of it becomes clear, and you observe them piercing into each other.'

'Do you remember this morning, when we visited the spring and the tiny pond of water, and I spoke of the Cross of the Incas? I asked the group if somebody saw it, and I listened to a voice answering me:

- I only find half of it.

'You were at my side and whispered me softly: 'the other half is reflected in the water.'

'You did notice it, he exclaims.'

- The water fascinates me. I answer.

- Precisely it is in the water, the one who has the solution, continues Jose.

'The union between the spiritual and the material is found in the water.'

'The particle of merger between what is corporeal and what is intangible is created in the water of our being.'

- Don Jose, I affirm, we have to seal this conversation and friendship with a toast of water. What you just communicate is extremely beautiful.

- But here in Cusco, it is yet more beautiful, because the only Company that has an exclusive deal with the water is Cusqueña beer, and we are forced to toast with it.

And Don Jose smiles with an expression of eternal happiness, and asks for some Cusqueñas.

- Only one for me, he affirms, I do not want to have too much sugar in the blood.

'Observe, he says, those people that could be watching us. We are speaking of something extremely interesting, private and hided; but it appears to them as somewhat strange, because neither is involved in our conversation, nor interested in the essence of the spirit. Our dialogue is at the same time, fenced, exposed and veiled.'

'We have had many meetings in Machu Pichu, in there, exhibited in front of them all, but we were invisible, as if we did not exist. We are the same as our Quechua culture, when you pierce our heart you discover a new Way.'

- Truly, the days here in Peru have been spectacular. I have found not my brother, but, I want to say farewell, in the same manner I would so do it with him.

- In what approach? Don Jose questions.

- So, I answer, laying my right hand on your heart.

- Do you know this was the Inca form of salutation?

- I was not aware of it, I replied surprised.

- They found mummies; and when buried them, they set their right hand on their heart and the left on the liver, which is the controller of the human body. And they did it in order that, in the world of the spirits, they had a lot of life and a bundle of love.

We stand up after the meal, and laying our right hand on each other heart, we departed.

I walked with Theo, back to the Hotel, through the porticoes of the Plaza de Armas.

Near the corner with Sol Street, my eyes perched on a painting. The look of the young girl attracted me persistently. I had never seen such penetrating, sweet and furious, cozy and repellent eyes.

I raised my eyes, while viewing the painting, to see the young woman selling it: it was a painting of her.

- You are the one in the picture! I exclaimed.

- Yes, she answered. Please buy his painting, she said pointing to an undernourished young man seated at the base of a column. He is a good painter; his friends call him 'the teacher'.

We bought the image.

The young man stretched out his hand to receive the payment.

- What is your name? I asked.

- Saul, he answered.

- It is a pleasure to know one of the best painters of the world, I said offering him my hand.

He presented his hand to me without saying a word.

As soon as I turned around, in direction of the Hotel, the vision of finding my brother came all of a sudden in front of me, I want to return, but an invisible force impels me, forcing my walk ahead.

I have found my brother.

'FOR ELISA'
From Beethoven

Manolo invented the Spanish word 'culpinos' (from 'culpa'), translated into 'blamers' (from 'blame'). The blamers are, according to him, those beings living in an intermediate state, between Heaven and Earth, in the obscurity of the world beyond, without their own light; nourished by our ailments, by our feeling of blame, guilt, culpability, fault, from where he formed de word 'blamers'.

Being a great clairvoyant, Manolo saw these gloomy individuals grabbing the physical bodies of their loved ones, bestowing on them all kinds of physical illnesses, that the human received as 'beneficial' or 'sent by God', thinking those sufferings were trials for their personal benefit.

Manolo used many hours explaining the erroneous human scheme of thinking when confusing these obscure beings with the ones of light, and when some sick person did not understand him, Manolo finished with these words:

- How are you going to understand me if you are filled up with 'blamers'?

And he closed the question mark with a smile, in which he left the people perplexed and without any possibility of contradicting him.

Those who knew Manolo spoke frequently of the blamers, and impute on them the reason of our accidents and ailments.

They feed on our sense of culpability, making us suffer, and it is in this, our agony, where they find their food and their strength.

If we keep ourselves below their dominion, accepting the ache and the blame, we are offering them a cuisine that they devour with such a craving that it is impossible to separate from us; and with their destruction, we receive more damage, until they finish wasting us completely.

The only technique to push them away from us is in living happy lives, removing from us the sense of blame and inviting them to search for the light, and so they may abandon us.

If I were to speak of this publicly the people will label me as 'strange' and 'obscurantist', therefore, my companions and myself prefer to abstain from naming them, because we already have too much with our work of identification of these spirits of blame to escape evasion.

Therefore it was compelling to me the other day when, visiting Elisa, she proposed them as topic of conversation.

Elisa is a free and wise spirit. Since we met, we connected, with no particular reason; in one of those big gifts that destiny offers us.

- When we begin the work of spiritual evolution, she says, we meet many visible and invisible enemies not desiring our advance. They covet eating of our misery because they cannot find the light. Why have you not spoken of them in your book?

- Elisa, I explain, you are opening a new chapter in our self-discovery, and I have to tell you that Manolo called these beings 'blamers', cataloging them like a group of dark spirits, related with us, since they were part of our lineage, and still they want to manipulate us.

- Manolo knew really what I am trying to tell you, she continues with her dissertation. These individuals, our familiars and friends, want to fill us with their feeling of blame; therefore he qualified them as 'blamers'. These beings want to be put in the center of ourselves to impede that we enjoy life. They are the ones who blame you in the mind, and they invent rules to subdue our spirits. They are those who have written our human history, with its eternal hate and loathing, with their desire of boring our existence and blocking our access to the light.

'When somebody makes you feel guilty, and saddens you, that internal ache is the food the blamer consumes in order to subsist in his sphere of enmity and destruction. And when in your loneliness they display to you feelings of blame, veer them towards felicity and freedom; but do not offer them the food they search for in you, because the more you give them, the most they demand from you and additional blamers stick to you.'

'Do search for your own internal development and independence and offer them the food of unselfish love, for them like a simple and insipid cucumber, or aromatic garlic that pulls out their hair with their bewitchment and fragrance.'

'Pursue for your felicity, self-government, delight and emancipation and you will help yourself and them.'

'The freedom of election offers you three possibilities: 'yes', 'no', and 'withhold'; if you say 'yes' or 'no' you are wrong, because where there are 'two' is always an enemy. If you do 'abstain' you select the best election, because you impose in yourself the norm of restricting your boundaries.'

'To say 'yes' or 'no', you succumb to a sense of blame of which you cannot be released. To keep yourself free and without fault, you must select the third possibility.'

'The third boost you up, and this is very important, it is not the union between the 'yes' and the 'no', it is a decision completely different and where the 'yes' and the 'no' cease to be found. To 'desist' is a free measure, incomparable and unique, that we have to search for in each situation of our life.'

'In the history of Adam and Eve we got this explanation: it comes an element from the outside, the snake, offering Eve, the mind, the possibility of eating or not the fruit. And the perception, as soon as it gives attention to this external forces, accepting or refusing the offer, whatever it may be its final decision, from the moment in which you offer a stranger the possibility of opening a gap between her and the spirit, between Eve and Adam, whoever it may be, she is already condemned.'

'So, it is not important to eat or not to consume of the fruit; looking at the fruit and choosing, it is to elude freedom, to open a crack in the internal and bite destruction.'

'The solution to the enigma it is to withhold and place boundaries on our freedom.'

'This is what, I think, says Elisa, you wanted to say in the 'stop', to curb the limits of your freedom, and be able to abstain of the election, avoiding the Fall; would that, 'to withdraw' would be 'to ascend.'

'Therefore, continues Elisa a little saddened, it is so difficult to make friends. There are lots of people reaching to your life offering you one thing or the other, and from the moment in which you select it, already you have an acquaintance. But they are not friends, because to be truly fond friends, you would have to abstain from making a decision, and accept them, not what they offer you, as a unique and permanent endowment.'

'When I had my first daughter, the nurse placed her in a cradle at the side of the bed. When they left me alone in the hospital, and I could rise up, I went to the crib and said to her:

- I do not know anything about mothers and you do not understand anything regarding daughters, and the two of us together need to learn.

'The doctor entered then, and he

listened to what I was telling my daughter, and until today he has it, engraved, written in his office.'

'Because this is a reality: we come here and know nothing about nothing, and we all have to grow together, or better yet, we got to love each other to grow together.'

'The children come to us in order that we teach them not what to eat or how to munch it, but feelings. We need to guide, to share our feelings with our children. For that reason they chose us, because they want our feelings, not our knowledge.'

'The people are scandalized because they confuse freedom with libertinism. Jesus was the absolute freedom and he had nothing of libertine.'

'For me, secures Elisa, there is only a sin and it is not to be happy. And in order to be content it is necessary to search for harmony. Therefore it is essential to put 'harmonic' limits, loving others as we love ourselves.'

'I think, asserts Elisa, that we can help these guilty, 'blamers' spirits, so they may find the light.'

'When we set order in our life, she continues saying, we are creating the rules of our own game. For example: I love freedom, but I always taught my children to put limits to that will, and each one of us must lay down the terms, so we will hurt nobody.'

'And this freedom gives you power to help others, not only physically, a minimum fraction of what we can do; but the aid must be mainly in the spirit, in which it multiplies, by a lot, our own small actions.'

'And they always give us small bits of taste to encourage us in our harmonic way of living. To me, primarily, they give me one cent; and cent after cent, I am kneading my spiritual fortune.'

'You, for example, gave me two, she secures.'

- I only remember of one, I say, the one which I found leaving your home.

- And do you not remember the one which you gave me parting from the restaurant? She questions.

- Oh, yes! Now I remember! I confirm.

'So be it, with two small cents, I continue saying, you already have enough to pay for the entrance in the Temple, as had the widow of the Gospel. And we are already here, fully immersed in the biblical thought.'

- Look at you, you are communicating to me something I did not think of before, answers Elisa.

'Although, she continues, the poor widow never attracted me, and her history was ignored by me, even though I always search for the tiny details in it all.'

'The Samaritan captures me persistently, and her dialogue with Jesus. That story is the essence of your book: searching for the inside source.'

- Elisa, I cut her short. saying, do not even move in there, because you have married already four times, and now you are becoming infatuated with one that it is not your husband.

- Ha, Ha, Ha... she laughs freely, as an answer to my intrusion.

- When people find their inside source, she continues, never complain or protest, they live their lives with a total felicity. And when these people turn around, to confront something, there is no way to alter them, because they have an internal security that is irrefutable. They are firm persons in their attitude.

'And they never threaten, she continues. They never announce what they are going to do, but on the contrary, they do it.'

'I always said to my son Aureliano:

- The things are not to be planned, but to be molded.

'Because, if you say you are going to

do it, or you are preparing to execute them, you never carry them out.'

FOURTH CANTICLE

ATTAINING THE HEART OF JESUS

THREE CRUCIFIXIONS

DOLORES

- They told me you have written a book, affirms a woman seated in a wheelchair.
- May I buy it? She investigates rapidly, without waiting for an answer.

Dolores, that's her name, bought the book and took it home.

I visited her some days later. She had an automobile accident two years ago, and presents her feet to me damaged, impeding her to walk. She pushes her wheelchair. She welcomes me with her great heart and her constant smile.

Her humble 'traila' includes a curtain dividing the small kitchen from the rest of the rooms. She is preparing beans for her family. The narrowness of the place pushed me outside.

- Please sit down, indicates with her kind voice tone.

I accommodate myself just at the door.

An intense feeling of wanting to do

something for her invades me, while deploring, my incapacity to carry it out.

- I would like to help you, I comment, take you to a doctor or, I do not know, to do something for you.

- To do something for me? She questions. I have lived all my life working. I woke up at five in the morning, prepared something to eat and went forth to the farm, after it, I went to clean houses, afterwards to the Packing Company; I returned home at ten at night to cook some food, chew it and put myself to sleep, and so, seven days a week.

'I worked, but did not live. I kept a husband and children, but I was so into my work and activity, than I never had time for them or me.'

'One night, I could not return home because of an accident. It was as if someone had set a 'stop' sign in my life, and I could move no longer.'

'When, after some days, they brought me to my humble home from the hospital, I discovered a new world. I did not know how my house was during the day, nor had I noticed the trees and plants so wonderful around me, neither the little birds, nor their songs.'

'Do something for me? She keeps asking. Before I was dead, I did not live, I only stored money to buy things for my children.'

'And do you know what? They never thank you for anything.'

'Everything I did for them was not enough, and I kept giving them more and added, and the extra I provided them, further they needed.'

'Do something for me? She reflects for herself. You already have done it with your book. Do you remember the passage in which you say that those who have feet remain immobile and the paralytics dance? This is my history. I controlled before my feet and I ran and hurried to do nothing. Now that I am paralyzed, I am born again, I see God constantly at my side, have time to dialogue with my children and educate them: to give them, not things, but my feelings as a mother.

- When I was small, it always ached me listen to the story of Cinderella. So much work and suffering, always cleaning out the same stuff, in order that these would get dirty again, and scrub them once more, and I kept asking myself for the reason of so much material misfortune.'

'After the accident I prayed and read the Bible, and tried to understand religion. But now, through the streaked letters in your book, I have discovered my soul.'

'I uncovered my treasure. And my fortune is love.'

'Each day I love more and more, no longer only my children, but the whole world, my love goes on extending without limits.'

'And, do you know what is to have no borders? It is the Infinite.'

'When you walk in love, your soul floods with so much happiness that you begin to dance, with sidereal ballets moving you to the Light.'

'My feet are destroyed. They have filled them with nails, maintaining firm my ligaments. So I am, as Jesus, fixed in my wheelchair.'

'When I read in your book that the paralytics dance, with these words I crossed to the Light, to Love, to Freedom. And I understood the plan of God: you have to stop to be able to ascend.'

'God works in the contradiction: the paralyzed walk; those who have feet they only move, but do not advance.'

'And I recognized the mystery of the Cross. Jesus, when fixed to the log is teaching us that at this time He Ascends to the Father.'

'Therefore the Cross is the essence of those who want to follow Him. Not a Cross that makes us kneel down and weep, lamenting our own wrong doings, but a Cross that it is a Door to another reality, towards Light, Love and Freedom.'

"In what way can you help me? She continues in her reflection. When I have learned from my experience, I will stand up from this seat of wheels, but not to have feet and move around and return to my old material work; and I would not even need my feet, because from my inside will sprout wings to fly to the Infinite.'

I, internally, wept when listening to so much beauty emerging from her poverty.

- Therefore, for me, the symbol of Christianity is the Cross and the Rose; because the Rose educates us, through the thorns, of the pain, to blossom beautifully. An ache that is not physical, but as indicated by the crown of thorns of Jesus, is a mental dissatisfaction.'

'When the mind finds herself lost and impotent, surrenders all its worth to the spirit, and this one is capable of harvest her with love, and transfer her, with him, to another territory, with beautiful dances, meanwhile the body stays fixed on the log.'

'Jesus, Dolores keeps saying, is the only one encouraging us, the unparalleled worker. All we, thinking to do a lot; we create nothing.'

'What you can do for me, she

answers to draw to a close, is to water this rose plant you have sown in my soul, so it may create beautiful red roses, that may be presented to the Father, in thanksgiving, for the much love He has for every one of His creatures.'

THE TEACHER

It was a hot summer day. I was seated at the side of the river, near John. The people arrived from every corner in order so he would look at them.

With lots of love and firmness, the eyes of John penetrated the most intimate of the being. There, he removed them from their inmost life, and with that uneasiness in their spirit, led them to the water and plunged them.

The beings, in their peace, remembered their past and glimpsed their future.

The summer invited us to swim and we spend a lot of time in the water.

The small group of his disciples helped him in his work, observing, from a distance, the constant awakening of each one of the entities.

The many, revering him as a prophet, brought him fruits and food. John shared it with all. As he distributed, it multiplied, and he satiated the crowd.

Some days a line of people shaped in their waiting, and John could not find time to rest. Other days, we hung around almost alone, without visitors, and John spoke to us about the world of the spirit.

His words were coarse and razor-sharp; he removed himself from the refinement of the oratory and of the big speeches. He preferred to act with his glance and without words, rather than with lengthy discourses.

John recounted recent events, the psychic situations of those who came to him, and with each human being, he offered the opportunity of connecting with their task, being at the same time unique and collective.

He prepared us morally in order that we might shape our own spiritual Way, and would not weaken in the attempt.

At his side, the days and months flowed rapidly. During the winter we searched for puddles of water to dip in, and briefly, because of the cold, we connected with our inside peace. With few disciples, his personality reached an unsurpassed tenderness, and his pupils, during the winter, adsorbed the best of him.

The summer was different. We employed our days in the water, the food was abundant, many came to him, and the cold stream of the Jordan refreshed the heat of the day.

One of those days, on returning from the waters, John joined us and said:

- The young man walking on the other side of the river is your Teacher, the one you must follow. With his access into the water I have seen His mission: He is the one who will take away the heaviness in all human hearts, removing the weight of blame, and then loading all in Him, the ailments of the humanity.

'With his immersion, I reached my zenith. I will surrender my body into the hands of The Most High, in order that in it, He would mold the consequences of all my terrestrial pilgrimage.'

'I will enter a period of loneliness and abandonment, and, even dough we will see each other again, I would not taste your company until we meet, again, all of us, in our celestial mansions.'

'I have given you a form of spiritual development in which I have set God above all things. All that we could find from what we qualify as 'heaven' downwards, everything are appearances.'

'Do not be deceived by them. Have God always at hand, and like fish that are living underwater, allow your heads to emerge at every moment, to breathe the pure air of the Almighty.'

'I have lots to tell you, but I will communicate it with my feeling. I am not happy as I reach my own liberation, because joy is a common good, and only when we gather again, my content will be complete.'

'My teaching is a preparation in order that you would understand this young man and become his disciples.'

He would not desire any farewell.

He walked in the distance, and we, following his indications, went after the young man to become His disciples.

In our society, we do not balance our lives, we are all incapacitated and in disharmony, with our brain divided in two, and not even using but a tiny fraction of it.

Those who do study sciences learn its laws, and they accept as certain what the professors communicate, without asking them why 2 and 2 are 4.

For those who study the arts, the procedure is completely opposite. There are also in our studies many laws to write, to paint, to produce a sculpture, to make a film.

But this education is different: on one side they force you to think and on the other edge they demand you to accept their form of reasoning, and it is here where the intelligent conflicts that change our society begin.

The artists ask: Who is the one who has written the number 2? Who is the one positioning the mark +? What is the meaning of the other 2? Who thought about =? Why do we have the number 4?

When we discover something scientific we are enormously cheerful.

But for the artists, to proclaim something philosophical or sublime, besides the same scientific cheer, share in bearing a rejection against the instructor directing you to an erroneous shortcut.

And, along with the joyfulness of the find, we feel a sense of contempt for the lecturer that pointed us to something different.

The bad professors are the most despised of all, when you realize their wrong doings.

I was an educator of philosophy, psychology, Latin, Greek and religion. So I am in the list of the 'undesired'. And I am pointing at it, because the base of our progress is to study.

There is an ingredient in the divine code so each one of us, in our inside being, we hold the secret of our own destiny and perfection; but this same Law of God, also bears that it is a stranger, somebody different to you, an outside force, the one promoting your awakening.

I do not know who initiated John, but I know it was somebody. John, however, awakened the Teacher. Each one of us wakes up through another human being.

The knowledge produces the change, not the books, the change simply is created by a look.

- Look at me!

The one who knows how to watch, therefore, becomes the best instructor.

John, for me, is excellently magnificent, but, following the teaching of this great instructor, the only one deserving the title of 'Teacher' is Jesus.

He came to coach us, but He used a master's form, through examples and parables, that He directed to our hearts, not to our minds.

Every one of His words is aimed at us, hence we may 'self-observe', and 'knowing' us, we may 'recognize Him'.

His teaching is completely different from the one of the school tutors. The professors educate us mentally. That is to say: what they impart to us goes directly to our reason, accordingly we may learn how to connect the electric joins, or build a house, or fashion socially. All of what we receive in the school, even religion classes, are directed to our minds, thus we may take notes, develop an idea and know how to work in this world we inhabit.

The Teacher, however, instructs in a completely different way. His parables go straight to our feelings. All that He communicates is bound for the heart. He aspires us so that His study could not be grasped by the mind, or the brain.

In this outline, those who believe themselves to be educators do not want to, nor can they accept His teachings, since these could not be expressed by the mind.

When we listen to His parables in our heart, these arrive at our essence.

Our mind, or thought, has not dominion over our feelings, and although we strive to waste His message, we cannot get it, since, moreover, it is written in the ether of this planet, and we may listen to it when we are capable of connecting with His spirit.

His words are so alive, they continue to stand and develop among the most advanced beings of our humanity.

His message, so much misunderstood at our mental level, is perceived in the horizon of the spirit like an enormous agitation, constantly 'in fashion'.

When you begin to move through your own personal path, you intersect instants of despair because you could not understand anything of what is going on around you, and you search for the door of access to other personal reality, and find yourself fenced in by bushes, like an animal that cannot get out of its painful prison, repressed and with fury, you try to clean out your jail, or dig an exit, in that process of despair, you are forced to bend towards the thickest of the shrubs, removing it with your own sweat, all stained with blood by its many thorns lacerating your hands; but you find, there hiding in penumbra, a hole of escape. It is so small that you can scarcely go through it and you have to diminish still more, only your skeleton can cross over, unwillingly you are compelled to lose each gram of fat, and already undernourished, slim, with your tunic of skin all bloodstained, you push yourself in through the obscurity of the openness, and extract your head beyond the mud wall. Only, then, you see the Teacher, surrounded by all the great beings of our humanity, all of them smiling to recognize you, and thrilled that another human being joining them.

There is a lot of joyfulness in that instant, only light surrounds you, all of them floating in the clouds, and on that moment you perceive your enclosure as a mirage of your mind, and to give it up, you observe it with love, because it has been the necessary instrument for your efforts and your work.

From wherever you are, the tactic of your thinking, your religion, your anti-religion, your atheism or deism, African, Asian, Polynesian, American, European or any dot on the planet: the reality of the spirit is given to you as One, it is only One environment, one yard, one prison, although having millions of mental diversities.

Then you understand the Word of the Teacher. You catalog His entire Gospel as alive. And it is in there that you perceive His parables as being, not only the indicating points of your walk, but also the ones guiding you through the eternal life of the stellar space. In our material level, the great majority of people criticizes them, hates them, and despises them. And if published, the books would be so unpopular, that no one would buy them, because the person reading this type of manuscripts cannot understand them; and if they were prepared to perceive them, they would be, as in the previous example, so obsessed in searching for an exit, they would not need them.

Therefore, the most of those who have found the door, already do not write, because they know that what it is annotated in the paper is useless.

That doesn't assert, that there is not, at this time, thousands of human beings, in this our mental, influenced and irresponsible society, millions of them are now trying to search for and to find the openness of access to the spirit.

Of what I am speaking of here, what the Teacher came to edify each of us, it is something reachable with the spiritual labor.

YAIRON

Yairon is a twenty-six year old young man. He has been imprisoned for seven years and next month he gets his freedom.

- Look at me, and listen, I have read your book and I have two questions.

- Just tell me, I answer.

- Explain to me about the human components.

- We may say that we humans have three ingredients, I explain him as a professor: the physical body, or the mind, the soul or the eternal thing in us and the spirit or the union between the divine and the carnal.

'In our human history many times the soul is identified with the spirit, or it is called as an inverted form 'spirit' to what is divine and 'soul' to the union with the carnal.'

'When you are born and go to school, your mind is programmed by your birth country, the religion you accept, the familiar history. So be it that your physical appearance, the color of the skin, the food you eat... all this is adapted to your present physical condition.'

'The soul, preparing its cover from another level, is incarnated little by little, shy and discreet, continuing with her eternal task arising from a status that she proposed to herself.'

'Paul, in his letters, encourages the followers of the Way writing to them: 'may your spirit, soul and body be transformed in Christ.'

'The Teacher, of brilliant form, it says that the 'Kingdom of the Heaven' looks like a woman placing a little 'yeast' in three measures of flour.'

'This idea, truly, it is from a great Teacher, because He doesn't qualify the three human components with the limitation of spirit, soul and body, but like 'three measures of flour', indicating with it that the three components have the same value, are equal, there is none of them superior or lower to the others.'

- Interesting! He answers me with a joking smile of assent.

- It is a Trinitarian unit, the one we posses in us, the one necessary to add a little yeast, a 'divine particle', in order that it may transform 'the whole', I continue trying to finish my lecture.

'The Fathers of the Church spoke of the 'Sperma Logos'. 'Logos' means 'Word', and 'Sperma' means 'Sperm'. They referred to God giving each human being, a particle infinitely small, a 'spermatozoid of the Word'. The 'Word' is Christ.'

'Every one of us receives a seed, a sperm, a little bit of yeast, a fraction of the Word we mix with the three human ingredients.'

'Therefore, I describe in my book, is the Divine arrangement of giving us constantly crumbs of bread, imprints of love, from the outside towards the inside, with a constant knocking, through the senses, in order that we open from our inside and may 'know ourselves.'

'The 'Kingdom of Heaven' looks like a merchant in fine pearls. And the pearl is what we are talking about: once you open from inside you receive one tiny stone, 'yeast', penetrating your being, and launching your transformation.'

'This is the 'Kingdom of Heaven'. The human components begin to be transformed at the same time as they cover with their light the pain that is seated in your being, and produces this oil, acid, DNA, luminous mother-of-pearl, our eternal treasure.'

'Although you are imprisoned and without freedom, you find yourself in the same situation as the remainder of the people. You are a being, not good or bad, not ugly or beautiful. You are an opaque and lifeless body, to the one constantly beaten from the outside until it opens.'

'And we always unlock with a kiss, a gesture emanating from the feeling of another human being, moving your heart, and you untie from your inside, receive your 'yeast', and initiate your complete transformation.'

'And it is so than, from within, you begin to undress, to remove each one of the cloths you have been accustomed to in your long evolution. And as you carry it out with your feelings, you do not pass judgment on anybody, but this same process gives you a faculty to love each human being and do not judge the situations so conflicting that afflicts them, since you, yourself have lived them.'

- I consulted many monks, and nobody has whispered to me what you are saying, says Yairon trying to arrange my sermon with his method of thinking.

- The work is comparable to an onion, I say: you remove cloak after geld, and you discover that this one, your deviate erroneous, has produced your defects; but with removing each pledge, you throw away your own faults and discover, when you reach to relieve the last one, that you are pure spirit, chaste air, virtuous light, a particle of God, a fraction of this Spirit we appeal as Father.'

'You were not, in the beginning, a sinner or saint, but a perfect atom of God, erring for a long time, and now making up your mind to walk to the future.'

'This personal and new light, each day, presents us small particles of light guiding us to the Infinite.'

'Search for in here, in the prison, in your life, these daily experiences illuminating your steps, for in them you will observe your past and your future, since the Father bestows on us constantly the possibility of knowing ourselves.'

'What I tell you, I continue, it is not to prove that I am special, or I have extraordinary powers, or that I know more than you, but on the contrary, what I communicate to you is common for each human being; we all can, and must, advance to the light.'

- And why do you call it 'the Way'? He continues asking me.

- I have not invented the name, I tell him, has been called that since the beginning. The Message, brought by Jesus, is an announcement of personal progress, to the one we qualified as 'the Way'.

'Naturally it has also common repercussions, but the gains cannot be achieved in group.'

- Here in jail we are forced to be part of a cluster, to feel protected, because if you are alone they destroy you, he explains.

- In every life situation you may be, they compel you to belong to a group, I manifest, not only here in prison.

- Maybe, this is the reason why the people that came at the beginning to your talks, do not want to get here now, he points.

- It may be so, I indicate.

- Moreover, keeps saying Yairon, do you think they understand what you are trying to tell them?

- Do you comprehend me? I investigate.

- A little, he responds, but that book of yours is very difficult to grasp. I have read it three times, and it is very complicated.

- Not, intricate it is not, I say contradicting; it is simple if you read it from your heart, but if try to analyze it, it is possible that you may find it entangled. But it was not my intention to cause headaches, but to encourage people in their personal development.

- But to nobody is it of interest, he

confesses.

- I already know it. You are here, I expose, because it pleases you to steal and drive expensive cars, others are here for different reasons, but I don't think those motives are their spiritual, but material growth. Have you learned something these years in jail?

- I did find out a lot of, he clears up. What I gathered is that is not worth the punishment to caress the fraction of happiness that it gives to steal and drive cars, when the punishment is seven years.

- Seven years for the robbery of a car? I ask.

- OK, they were several, he adds smiling. I was a confirmed thief preparing his redemption. But do not switch the conversation and continue your talk on spiritual work.

- Therefore, I further explain, this labor of the spirit is painful, to the effect that it is necessary to communicate it from one to one. It cannot be done in groups or in common. Neither can be forced. It is an arduous and rough task, because the stone, hiding from its creation, rather prefers the passivity and the obscurity, than to discover itself as the flint and announce its own light.

'Consequently, the Teacher repeats in the Gospel about the process of spiritual growth to remain secrete or private.'

- Here in jail we cannot have, nor there are, any secrets, exposes Yairon.

- All of humanity despises this remark, but the word 'secret', has for Jesus a different meaning. For Him it expresses 'spirit'. The Teacher addresses the development of our psychic energies. In the same way the process, the teachings, the work, the labor of the human being must be developed intimately, without this procedure being understood by the flesh, by the human mind.'

'We are beings sweating in two realities: the material and the spiritual one, but we are one and cannot wear away of this Unit. Therefore when we carry out something, small as it may be, it is, at the same time, physical and psychic.'

'The operation must be made here, in the corporeal, with our mental tool, but guessing that our labor is not only solid, but also ethereal. And the absolute director is our soul, not our mind.'

- That is too complicated for me, says Yairon, allow me to reflect on it and I would get back to it some other day. Now talk to me of what is the most important of my discoveries in your book.

- And it is? I ask him.

- The evolution of the soul from one

country to the next.

I remain perplexed for a few seconds. From all the people commenting the book, only Yairon attained this idea.

- How intelligent you are, I comment, you have been the only one asking me on that. Now I see clearly that you are a great thief of cars. You are so intelligent, and at the same time so stupid in order for them to catch you.

- So it is life, he confesses resigned.

- What do you want me to explain? I insist on my question.

- Well, first about the child of twelve. Did you truly saw him later as an adult?

- Yes, so it was.

- What I liked the most in your book is when they explain you that dream, bit by bit. What a great thing for me.

- It pleases me, I answer.

- Now, about Pontius Pilate, when he decides to migrate to Poland with his group. Explain it to me.

- Do you understand, from your prison, what it means 'to be free'?

- Of course I know, he responds

- In the spirit it happens exactly the same, I answer.

- Explain it.

- You are a prisoner here, and you tell me they impel you to be part of a group.

- Yes.

- Equally in your spirit: you are imprisoned and they incite you invisibly to integrate into different groups.

- Are you trying to say, that these rods are not only palpable but also immaterial?

- In effect. Just as you do join a group, your spirit sticks to other spirits in tune with you.

- Then freedom does not exist? We can never get it? He inquires with insistence.

- Beloved Yairon, I answer, what an intelligent question. You are truly extremely intelligent, because in your inquiry you are giving me the exact reply.

- Of what are you talking about?

- Do you remember the evangelical story of the crucifixion of Jesus, with the two thieves?

- And now you place me as crook? He claims smiling.

- This is exactly what you are teaching me, I clarify.

- The two thieves, already crossing to another level, discuss among themselves, insulting Jesus because He is between them.

'They impute Him, the failure of Jesus, the uselessness of His doctrine, which cannot save them, nor bail out Himself.'

'Because by the simple act of being in

the center, among them, He finds himself abandoned by all and without a group that assists Him, neither in this material level nor in the intangible one.

- Now I understand, says Yairon. The 'good thief' perceives that they, the crooks, are paying for their guilt; but the situation of Jesus is different. He is atoning for nothing.

'To be in the center, in the heart, is to suffer for some reason that does not belong to me, but it is a common wealth, a fortune belonging not to any of the factions.'

'And, on the other hand, the two groups want to get it, but cannot obtain it.'

'The answer to all these questions is Love.'

'Love is what these opposite groups neither have nor can get it, because they search only for followers to their cause, members increasing in numbers the row of companions, but any of these groups worries about the individual, are not concerned for the essence, do not care for the uniqueness.'

'And then the 'good thief' leaves his group, and in there, crucified and without the possibility of moving, says to Jesus:

- Remember me, when you arrive at your kingdom.

'And Jesus answers him:

'Really I say to you, since now you

are with me in Paradise.'

'The 'good thief' chooses to be in the heart, in the hub point.'

'But this core place is not the intermediate summit between two components. The position of the heart is individually completely different and unique, not being part of any of the two, and however, His presence, destroys them.'

'What I am declaring you is so great, continues Yairon, that I have to reflect it over.'

'Since I was a tiny altar boy, I listened to all these histories, but now, thanks to you, I understand them.'

- It is just the opposite, I tell him, and you are the one revealing them to me.

- Allow me to return to my question. Then there are two levels, the material and the other. The two of them manifest themselves equally. I do want to say that there is not freedom in this world or in the world to come.

- Yairon, I say, your question reveals the answer. These two levels arrayed in order, one to the other, they imitate each other. The spiritual is an image of the physical or the corporal object is a portrait of the spirit. But what you are teaching me is that the energy of Jesus, when you take His hand, is the one impelling you to a third level, beyond the spiritual, grafting you to the pure mysticism.'

- Continue with your explanation, in relation to my question, he insists.

- What I have seen in my night vision is that Pilate, following his thinking of service to a cause that he named 'the Roman Empire', would crave to keep that Empire forever, beyond the grave, and he invited his followers to backtrack his cause, and they moved to Poland, and from there planed the reconstruction of the Empire.

'But this, I continue, is very private and secret for me, and I only wrote about it in the book, showing a thread of world history, crossing, in an outward appearance, the human tapestry, and leaving vestiges in the whole planet.'

- Do you want to say that we all move in groups, following common destinies, even when we cross over to other world, reflects Yairon.

- In effect, I recognize. And what you just showed me is this: grasping Jesus hand, we may walk finding a middle point between two opposites, and attain a new level.

- And do you know of another group? He questions again.

- Certain people rumor about the souls of the ancient Athenians moving to

France; the Spartans to Germany; therefore the friction between these two nations, conveying the effects from their old disputes. It explains, though, the French interest for philosophy, and the German inclination for sport and physical beauty.

- And the old Romans are they still in Rome? He inquires

- Not, I clarify; it is rare that a human being be born twice in the same place. The actual Romans incarnated there, searched for the spirit of their forefathers; as in each country. The people pursuit for what others dropped, thinking it may help them in their development, but we all move following our own freewill and desire. And so, the ancient Romans, they say, are the English of today.

- 'All roads lead to London', he intervenes with cunning.

- Maybe for other people, I say. But for me, today, you have revealed me a great secret.

- Truly?

- You are an altar boy, so intelligent having escorted me to the Third Heaven. Accompanying you to your heart, you have shown me the Way. Besides being intelligent you are a great thief.

- Why?

- Because you stole my racing car and went speedily and surely to Paradise.

Searching for what you had embezzled, I followed you and went very far away.

- But, adds Yairon, following with your suggestion, they cut the legs of the crooks so they could not walk in the other world.

-Yes, I specify, you are pardoned, but not reformed, you continue being a great thief.

- Soon I will get out of here, he indicates, and I would like to continue our conversation.

- You are extremely intelligent, but, I say smiling, your dialogue proves to me that you still are not regenerated, and I do not know if you will get out of here.

FIRST INSERT FROM THE SPIRIT

MANOLO
It is a nickname for
MANUEL
Hebrew/Aramaic word meaning:
GOD IN US

MANOLO

- Manolo, I ask, can you tell me something in reference to sex?

- The sex last until you are tired of it, he responds.

'When you develop spiritually, everything changes in your life.'

'Your instincts, not controlled by your spirit, are manipulated by the collective unconsciousness, and if you leave them to act by themselves, they produce in you a moral lethargy and in 'passive form' you act 'like the rest'.'

'You are part of the great human bulk, circulating with the daily monotony we impose on each other by work and social relations.'

'This order of things has not any moral value, positive or negative, an apathetic mass, irresponsible, governed by any mental spasm caused from the exterior.'

'But, when you begin your tiny spiritual walk, there is a force in you impelling to evade this great amorphous agglomeration, so you may detach from it, and search for your own door of exit to your heart.'

'When you are part of the crowd, you are, as all: procreator. As animal, it sprouts from you these sexual instincts, manipulating the humans.'

'They educate you to cover your nakedness, and so others could not loathe the sight of your flesh.'

'The same as everyone else, society forces you to marry and beget family: you are a procreator.'

'We humans behave the same as the animals, attracted towards the magnetism of sex.'

'In older times, at the beginning of our development here on earth, we conducted ourselves following a stellar guidance. The people united in the spring to have children, and they were born in winter. In the life of Jesus, where all is perfect, it occurred in this way. But nowadays, when breaking all natural order, we force the sex daily.'

'When I was child, backing up not even a hundred years, the cats and dogs had sex once or twice a year. Nowadays, as they imitate us humans, the animals have sexual intercourse almost daily and the number of cats and dogs multiplies in a chilling form.

And this is from imitating us humans, in our disharmonized manner of behaving.

'It is necessary to allow the development of these animal tendencies in the humans; to educate them, yes; but not to repress them.'

'The parents must inform their children on sexual matters, and with their feeling, help them so these animal tendencies sprout from them in harmonic form. But they should not repress these tendencies, and much less, search in religion for the method of this repression. Therefore, I am not pleased on the religious instruction of children, because they cannot, at that age, extract what they do not have yet in themselves.'

'Looking back to the life of Jesus, we could say that spiritual development begins about the thirty years of age'.

'Nowadays, we are all in a hurry, we could move it from the twenty-one to the twenty-six years. In that time we should search for our Way towards the spirit, but not before. Since when you are a child, you do not know which way to go, nor in what place to search for.'

'The religious instruction you have received, has not touched your inner self, you have to discard it as useless, and this, truly, is a pity.'

'But, if around the twenties, you do conquer the reins of your own doing, you penetrate a world opposite to all procreation: it is the realm of creation. You become a creator.'

'These things of the spiritual world are not for the majority of the people, but for those who are little married, divorcees or bachelors.'

'Ha, Ha, Ha…', he laughs happily.

'It is a shame I did not study more the life of Buddha, because he is a very special being. But the little I know of him, is that he was married and with children, and when he discovered his essence, he gave up his spouse and family, and crossed to the light.'

'Jesus neither married'.

'In my years I have seen many people trying to access the spiritual world, and I have seen that for those who are very married, it is almost impossible.'

'Well, if you are little married; that is to say, that you do marry, but do not give you too much importance to marriage, but this one is a form of life in which you are not too much in love with your spouse; and you have children, but you are not excessively on them, trying to atrophy them, but simply protecting them with your love and giving them feelings to guide them and award them stability in their lives; then, that one finding yourself little married, allows you to move freely in the spirit.'

'If you are single, you are freer. If you are divorcee and already went through it all, then, I have seen it many times, you may imbue in this world of the spirit and begin to create.'

'And to create is not to form a new body. Creation is to love what already has been created and loved.'

'When you care for those old things anew, cleaning out the accumulated dust caused by the abandonment, and you increase the affection given in the past; and this one recent tenderness, getting them healthy, caressing and kissing them, is hoping for the moment in which they will open from the inside, and may be manifested in the flesh.'

'You are not a procreator, but, just as the Teacher, creator.'

- Manolo! I say
- Yes? He questions
- Why do I get the impression of not catching you wholly, and not understanding your talk?
- Because you do not comprehend me, he responds.
- And why?
- Because it is so.
- Explain me a little better what you

just said, I ask him.
- What is the topic of our conversation?
- About marriage
- And what do you understand of what you just heard?

I repeat again, word by word, all his teaching, to prove that I am a good pupil and I learn the lesson very well.

After my long reply, he answers me:
- There it is.
- What do I get? I return to ask him.
- That you understood nothing
- Don't I?
- I am not talking about marriage, he clears up, I am discoursing regarding you.
- And?
- Let us suppose that you are God and you are going to judge all the dogs of the world. And I ask you, as Supreme Being that you are and creator of those animals: Are you condemning them or saving them for a reason if they procreated or not?
- Manolo! I answer, if that is an absurd! How am I supposed to condemn a dog for having or not sexual relations? It is an intrinsic law in the nature of the animal to reproduce. I cannot base my judgment going against the same laws I have created.
- Precisely, he responds me.
- But what does this has to do with

me?

- That is the root of the solution: I am talking to you, the given example is for you. Do you think that God is passing judgment by the children we have, or if we are married or single?

- Well, that is what Jesus said in the gospel.

- And do you understand Jesus?

- Not too well, I recognize.

- No, he fixes, you do not know Him at all. Jesus is not speaking about nature; here in this atmosphere, you have to behave as animal that you are. Jesus is talking about another superior orb, where the moral laws are different.

- Who may guess Jesus? I investigate.

- The one who analyzes well His words.

- And who may perceive you, Manolo?

- The one who reflects what I say.

'Look at this, he continues, in this level that we are, we all have to bear according to the decrees established by the Creator. These laws cannot be altered, and when you find the Truth, you do not even dare to try to differ an apex from them.'

'These codes don't need to be implemented. Our world is perfectly established just as it is.'

'I am not telling you about this existence, but regarding another degree.'

- Explain it to me a little more, I ask.

- In the previous case, in which position do you find yourself in?

- As a bachelor, since I never been married.

- Incorrect answer.

- Why?

- Because you are married and with a heap of children.

- Am I?

- Of course you are, he insists. The marriage of which I am talking has nothing to do with carnal intercourse or the marriage we caress in our society. The example is referred to you, stuck to an idea, and that is the wedding you must separate. You have to divorce your own thoughts, ideas or obsessions.

- My blue print is Christianity.

- Precisely, he says, there you have it. You have to nullify this living together with your idea.

- But how I have to do it? I ask him.

- The 'how', I cannot give to you. But I have to encourage you to divorce your philosophy.

- Then it will be as giving up the Teacher.

- Precisely the opposite, he continues.

'You cling to the Christian idea, marry to it, and you think your concepts are going to save you.'

'But the Teacher is not the idea. The Teacher is. And you got to divorce the idea and follow the Teacher.'

'Therefore you must give up your philosophy, and search only for a man, a human being.'

'The marriage is perfectly placed and founded; it is a fraction of this world.'

'Of what Jesus speaks, and I am repeating, it is in relation to a level where philosophical principles, the ideas and the human flows of thought disappear; and only people are found, but not beliefs.'

'The ideas are fictitious, and see how many have sprout out of Jesus' so called disciples, believing they are tied to the instruction of the Teacher and they hate each other, with thousand of preachers not knowing what they are saying, and none of them understands, or loves Him.'

'And there are millions of wives.'

'The sex, for example, is another spouse, a different belief, another philosophy, taking you to boredom; and just imagine how many millions of peoples are moored to this philosophy, writing books, filming, marrying, not with a human being, but with the philosophy of sex.'

'The same thing happened to me. I began to cure people. Do you know how beautiful it was? When I could see someone sick with Aids, I gave him some plants and cured him, and I felt so happy. I was married with the medicine.'

'Afterwards I noticed that nothing served for nothing. The people searched for me, not because they wanted to be healed, but as a plaster, that cured momentarily their illness, but the crowd wants to continue matched to their form of thinking, without any desire of changing.'

'Each illness is caused by some wrongdoing. When they came to see me I tried them to discover their own imperfection, but did not achieve it. It has been a handful of people, those who have seized me, in the spirit, and have been healed forever.'

'The majority were relieved for a few days, they returned to their feeble routine, and set back to their ailment to die in it.'

'I thought I did something for them, but I accomplish nothing. I had to divorce myself from the medicine, and allow them to die, and they expire because they are ignorant persons, because they are unable to search for the 'why' of their illness, and find a path to solution.'

'And it is not only succumbing as sick

persons, but when dying, and moving to the next level, to an inferior spiritual degree we may qualify as mental, they continue as sufferers, and it is in there where they have to go to school, to eliminate the mortal stains scrutinizing them. These tarnishes are much more dangerous than the material ones.'

'In this flat level we find ourselves in, all of it is tiny; in the mental world all is excessively enormous.'

- In that case we cannot help anybody, I assert

- Do you help somebody? He asks me straight on.

- I believe I do, with meetings and chatters.

- Again, the wrong answer. The people listening to you is a crowd married with an idea, and they go to you, so you may, in turn, gild the image, cover it with chocolate; and, as they like chocolate, they accept it as the supreme truth.

'But since the first moment, in which the group belongs to a philosophical current, is tied, working for its spouse and children; their mind functions for the company for which they toil.'

'But none of them cares for you. They do not want you, nor accept you. You are only an instrument they use and abuse for their own pleasure, but you are nothing to them at all, therefore they will draw you out when you say something unpleasant or are disagreeable with them.'

- Jesus already said that His disciples would be dragged out from the Synagogues, I point.

- The Teacher is saying to His disciples: they will push you out from the spiritual Synagogues; it is always of that world, of the one, which He speaks.

'But, listen to me, he continues, I am telling you something more. It is not the clan pulling you out of the corporation. What I say to you is that you must generate a spiritual force to depart, by your own will, and leave them.'

- And so give up, thus they may be misled? I insist.

- But they are already discarded and useless by the simple reason of belonging to a group, he responds to me.

'How many times, the Teacher, after healing somebody, would say:

- Do not even enter into your people.

"We are given the possibility of working here, since in that other sphere, the toil is much more difficult and complicated, and it would take a lot to advance. Here, a tiny step represents a great stretch in the spiritual level.'

'The Teacher is of that universe, the

one of which He speaks. Of this material reality are the taxes, the currency and Caesar. We display rage, when we try to waste His teaching, lowering it to levels purely vulgar, clumsy and coarse.'

- Then? I ask him.

- Then, when you divorce from your philosophy, you do search for a 'being', and, when on finding him, this one human being will lead you beyond the ideas, to the pure world of the soul.

'You turn into a vagabond, without country, or family; you become disinherited; and attain freedom, divorce, anarchy in the spirit, training you not to destroy, but to build your country estate.'

'It is then when you love, truly. You do love a human being, not ideas. And, loving, you develop into becoming a creator.'

- I do not understand this, I say.

- That is the reason why I am saying it to you, in order that when you get it, you may know that I already have said it to you.

- And why do I take so long to understand it?

- Look! Some people take longer, others grasp it fast. I have seen you in a remote past. From Atlantis you are trying to get it.

- So much time? I ask him brokenhearted

— But I have to tell you also, he continues, that I have seen you naked. So continue on your pledge.

SECOND INSERT FROM THE SPIRIT

THEO
It is a nickname for
THEOPHILUS
Greek word meaning
BELOVED BY GOD

THEO

- My name is Theophilus, meaning 'lover of God', but you may call me 'Theo', connoting 'God', he said to me, smiling, the first time we found each other, many years ago.

Theo has taken part in many of these encounters. And with him, I am searching for this third magnetic sphere proclaiming and explaining our spiritual progress.

Well, if you ask him, he will report these findings in a different fashion and even in a contradictory proposition.

These stories, projecting from his mouth, he will embellish with more color and life, lengthening them endlessly and exposing quantity of minute details.

But this is normal and worthy of praise, since each one of us has his own eyes, ears, mouth, hands, nose, mind, spirit and as much as component there is, and therefore we perceive colors, music, flavors, feelings, aromas, mental forms, spiritual or elementary magnitudes from different viewpoints.

And I am very happy that it is so.

I ask Theo to explain his Way to me.

- I am, he says.

- What are you referring to?

- My name is Theo, 'God', and the name of God is 'I am'.

'Just look at Moses, he continues, he steals his people out of Egypt, robbing, moreover, the whole gold and the spiritual Egyptian philosophy.'

'His followers ask him in the name of what god, he is carrying out all these quests.'

'Moses goes to the desert, and in there, he asks God for His name.'

- My name is 'I am', answers God.

- And? I ask Theo in order that he develops his idea.

- And 'I am' is the name of God. For me this story is one of the most beautiful of all the human chronicles.

'As all the human beings have a particle of God, that divine seed is called 'I am', and it is found in every one of us.'

'Do you know what it means?'

'Each one of us is 'I am', and you have to accept each human being as God. It doesn't matter how he or she is dressed, or the money they hold in the bank, or the gold bunching around their neck, everyone is a fraction of God, and you cannot love God, if you do not love each one of His creatures.'

'When you take conscience of 'I am', the whole world falls to your feet, and you receive all the riches of humanity.'

'Because, following with the history of Moses, they melt down the whole of Egypt's gold to represent God as a bull, and Moses wasted it as useless, losing all the stolen wealth.'

'The revelation of the 'I am' has far more value than that of all the Egyptian opulence.'

'But what it is going on?'

'Down here we all behave like the old Israelites, working physically and stealing from each other, to store gold. We do not balance the material task, producing only possessions and at the end, all of it is destined to the recycling.'

'Our assignment is to discover the 'I am', and that finding only occurs when you unmask the 'I am' residing in others.'

'Therefore, when the old Jewish refuse to understand Moses, this one destroyed the dispositions of 'I am', he went up again to the mountain and supplicated to the same God, that He would write new decrees, for a low kind of people, spiritless and dull.'

'He offered them the Ten

Commandments, engraved in stone, in their brain, in their mind, since this people could not accept superior forms of conduct.'

'The revelation of Moses, is not therefore an 'edict', thought primarily to organize a material people; but on the contrary, a prophecy of the 'I am', freeing an openness to a higher reality.'

'The Divinity revealed herself in the Messiah when installing, at an assortment of times, her development in us:

I am the Way
I am the Truth
I am the Life
I am the Good Shepherd
I am the Door
I am the Light of the World
I am the Grapevine
I am the Resurrection

'The development of the soul grows in peculiar way in each human being. It is erroneous to sort step by step, as many do, the spiritual stages, since each one of us moves distinctly.'

'What hindrance the most our personal advance, is to self-encase, become a fraction of a group, speculating what convoy shelters each other, when in really the community has not life in itself, it is a heap of ideas founding an organization; and the concepts and rudiments change constantly, and they are, moreover volatile and develop in unforeseeable and anomalous system.'

'Then the classification exists: they want to catalog you and give you a name, an identification number, country, race, iris of the eyes and an unbelievable quantity of squares in order that you fill them with your favorite color, your desired book, your unforgettable film... and a quantity of pedantries.'

'Afterwards they copy the report in the computer, they store you inside there, and already they have your chip.'

'The lump of the modern centuries, with absence of intelligence, is crushing.'

'They assume that having my data already control me because they know where I have been.'

'But they fail because they do not care about me, nor they know my future.'

'But in our society everyone has an eagerness of ruling others, which it is a social and contagious illness, worse than leprosy.'

'Who gave to the people the idea of controlling others and to be leaders, or to be the number one?'

'I am a heartily Buddhist and I have to respond: the eagerness of desire.'

'Buddha taught a Way, searching in

your heart for the root of the desire, and eliminating it, to extirpate your pains and sufferings.'

'For me the worse desire is the one of mastering others. Why do we want to make proselytes of our form of thinking, and drag the people towards a utopia?'

'We do not get salvation being the poppa, the mamma, the sister or brother of Tarzan. Redemption is a private and personal Way, where it matters nothing, your carnal or physical relation, and a lot, your work as spirit searching for light.'

'The only temptation we have is to let us be dragged along by ideas or concepts enslaving and killing us.'

'There are no more important people for me than the one who serves.'

'They teach me how to fix myself in life and to search for the dots of light in my existence, and I know, that following these people, I cannot fail, since they direct me with firm steps through the path of kindness.'

'And I revolt against any program of personal development, because none of them is useful.'

'Life itself may somewhat present you very advanced notions at a tender age, and on the ripeness of your existence somewhat appearing more immature.'

'The Teacher gave us in the 'I am' the spiritual stages in which we develop as human beings.'

'In the Beatitudes, the necessary qualities for our entrance in the superior worlds are announced:

- To be poor in spirit, that is to say: needing breath.

'The spirit, or air, is common to all the humanity. We inhale and the breath penetrates our lungs; we exhale it and it returns to the common blizzard.'

'We may not take possession of it, since it does not belong to us, and if we should say: this Spirit or sigh is mine, and keep it for more than five minutes, we would die.'

'The Air we inhale gives us life, and we exhale it, after penetrating in us, returning to the common wealth, loaded with our sufferings and ailments.'

'The same Ether we share it with the plants, animals and the remainder of the human beings. In less of a week crosses the planet, inundating life to all it caresses.'

'Poor in spirit means to know our respiration as universal, not belonging to us, we cannot make it ours, it is necessary to share it, let it go out; and ask for it, again, to the Father, so He may provide constantly for our breathing.'

'If you work on this conduct of poverty of spirit, the Teacher says, the Kingdom of Heaven will be yours.'

- Another attitude is the mildness, meekness or tameness. In Spain you got the 'halters' or 'meek', they are bulls, already older and expert, that with smoothness and certainty, direct the young ones.

So be it the character of the meek: to become experts in the world of the spirit, and with only your presence, guide with smoothness, certainty and kindness, the ones that need it, knowing that they walk towards their martyrdom or destruction, but what is important is to be at their side, besides the one needing you, without saying a word. Only your presence is necessary.'

'If you do so, you will inherit the Spirit of the Earth.'

- Another attitude is to weep. To moan wanting to change something, and not to be capable of executing it, when trying to throw down so many walls surrounding the human feelings and impeding them to flower; you sympathize with furor, because you cannot compose the labor, that must be carried out by each human being, and you do lament of impotence and moan. If you do so, you will be consoled, not in this deteriorating world, but in the zephyr inundating you.'

- Another to develop is to be hungry and thirsty for Justice. Not human scrupulousness, blind fairness with a sword, but Divine equality, with Light and Peace. You do get an appetite and craving for Divine Integrity, and you will perceive each human being paying for what they owe: thus the reason why we all are born incapacitated, in one way or another.'

'And the Father will reveal to you 'the why' of human miseries and the value of His Justice, so opposed to our human courts, and your gluttony and vehemence will be satisfied.'

- Be merciful with others, and the Father will show you His compassion.

- Do keep a clear conscience, and do not darken it with defamatory actions, neither with lies dim it, nor swaddle it with the impure habit of the egoism, do not disturb its august serenity with your lower passions. In it, says the Teacher, you will see God.

- Become a pacifier and you will be called Son of God.

- When you suffer the persecution and the hate of the powerful, for your ideal of Justice and Brotherhood, to free the humble from their slashing and slavery, then lift up your head and cheer up, because your Redemption is near.'

'This is the Way: to see God in others, and in observing Him, you grow internally; God becomes present in you.'

'Throw away your ideas and theories and accede to that fellow man you find in the street, rejected and refused by many, speaking of God in a clear, certain and sure form.'

'Ask them, who is God, and their answer will be true.'

'Each human being is 'I am'.'

'In the same way, 'I am' is each human being.'

- Who are you? They ask the Teacher.
- 'I am', he answers.

'They crash down when listening to His answer, are scandalized because He uses the name of God, the 'I am.''

'In the same manner our society howls when stumbling with a subject, imputing on him all kinds of tares, incapacities and ballasts.'

'Thinking that we worship God, we insult each other and degrade ourselves.'

'Really we are fighting against the Divinity, when we so regard each other.'

'We have to accept the 'I am' just as he is, knowing him covered with quantities of rags, seized along his pilgrimage.'

'But deciphering his 'I am', allows him to undress, remove his clothes and discover the Divine essence in himself; and we will understand that we all are lovers of God, and therefore gods. We are 'Theo'.'

'And when reaching the heart of God you will utter:

'I am Love.'

FIFTH CANTICLE

GATHERING PRECIOUS STONES

THREE STORIES WITH LOTS OF GEMS

PACO

Lola invited twenty-one people to the presentation of my book in Algemesi. Some of them were known to me, others not.

- Paco! One of them introduces himself, affirming his attendance.

- Vicente! I answer, giving him my hand.

During the presentation, Paco leafed anxiously through the pages of my book searching for some bibliographical reference, to ascertaining from where I brought so many ideas from.

- They are dreams, I said to him desiring to erase from his mind the oppressive anxiety of hunting for references.

- Ah! Hum... I already see it... because of the title... and for the 'hippie' cover page.

However Paco continued, in the background of his mind, rummaging around for a solution to his question.

- Who has given you so much freedom of expression? Is not your superior controlling you? Does he not read what you write?

- What leader, I answer, is interested in the spirituality? The only matter incumbent for them is the material property.

Paco returns to his brain panting to find the origin of my knowledge, in the meanwhile leaving others to take part in the questioning.

During the chatter, the subject of reincarnation was introduced in a natural form.

At the end of the presentation he approached anew to affirm his belief:

- I do not believe in reincarnation! He asserts definitive. What does all that mean? He questions with curiosity branding to those present.

Theo, at my side, utters:

- Are you the teacher and do not know it?

A few of the people present, opened their mouth in unison, surprised when listening to Theo's question.

- Why these chill when snooping to this verdict? I ask.

- Do you not know who he is? Manifests Lola. He is Paco! The theologian.

I considered Paco to be the best theologian of Valencia in the present time. I did not know him by sight, and his introduction did not descry anything else about him.

- Are you the famous Paco, the best theologian of Valencia? I ask him.

- Are you a theologian? Are you the best theologian of Valencia? Adds also Miguel, one of the other's present.

- If he says so..., answers Paco.

- Have you read any of my books? He investigates.

- Of course, I depose. But just look at what precisely happened here. You direct to me a question, and Theo responds to you with the same words the Teacher directed to Nicodemus.

- Nicodemus, I clarify in my explanation to the audience, was not a teacher in Israel, he was 'the' teacher of Israel, the best instructor treasured by the nation on that moment. And at night, what is curious, now that I am expressing it, 'at night', I revoked the affirmation, during sleep, in his dream, that has not any importance for you as scholar, he visits Jesus and asks Him the same question, on the reincarnation.

- I do not understand what you are telling me, admits the teacher of Israel to the Universal Teacher. How can an old man enter his mother's womb and be born again?

- What is born of the flesh, is flesh,

reveals the Teacher; what proceeds from the spirit, it is spirit. Do not be alarmed when I tell you that you have to reincarnate. The wind blows where it wants and you do not know where it comes from or where it goes. So it is with everyone born from the spirit. If you are not born again, you cannot enter the Kingdom of Heaven.

- Can you take me to Valencia? He interrupts when seeing me gathering all my belongings in order to leave the conference room.

- Of course, I secure.

- I would not want to be in that car, some of those present said jokingly, because sparks will come out in your conversation.

And they were not wrong, but they fell short, because no sparkles came out, but Light.

During the half hour of the trip he exhibits his extensive work.

- Do you know how much I have sweat, suffering to approach the Primitive Church, and the original Christian Way of thought? And you come in a second, and without any consideration either to traditions or to your superiors, you plunge fully into the Original Christian Way of Life. You are acting as Jesus: it is not that He treated the high priests wrongly, but He behaved as if they did not exist, as if they had no importance. And you are doing the same thing. I find myself furious with you for speaking in a form so simple and plain, about some truths, for me, so difficult to utter.

I, abhorring flattery, was receiving one of the greatest ovations.

- And you have put it, moreover, in form of dreams, so no one can refute you.

I smile pleasantly when seeing the theological teacher of Valencia piercing beyond the mind, lighting up his light in the spirit.

- All my books address the same topics, extends Paco: the Original Church, one with my love for Jesus and His doctrine.

'The one who wasted it all was Constantine and his partisans. He was tired of fighting against the Christians, because they had not religion, temples, dogmas, or altars. They gathered at home privately and spoke of Jesus, remembered Him with love, they lived with the same feelings.'

'And here comes Constantine, gathering the bishops in Nicea, the Pope did not attend, and he told them to make out of Christianity a religion as any other, to have Jesus as God, as it was the Caesar, to get altars and donations, and to give up those primitive ideas, and form a religion as the other devotions of the world.'

'And do you know what? Insists Paco, all gave him a free ride.'

'Constantine asked to kill Pope Sylvester, and with him died the original Way, to create the clumsiness of the present Christian religion, with many believers, but without Jesus.'

'We have allocated Jesus, as if He was for ever impotent and crucified on the Cross, with His hands fixed on the log, in order that He could not embrace us.'

'How furious I am with you, that, without bothering about nothing, you have launched yourself fully in the arms of Jesus, without considering the absurd tradition that goes by roundabout each other.'

- Do not be angry, Paco, I also pained and worked, and myself, as well have read a lot, but I did become aware of the true history we hold within our hearts; and the chatter you just gave us, it has been the best presentation about the subject I have received ever. Truly you are the professor of Valencia, persevere in your labor, because Jesus is at your side, and He will never give up on you.

'In reference to the reincarnation, I continued saying, Jesus has come to teach us the end of Reincarnation. He ratifies us that we had enough reincarnations, because we are not gaining anything living once and again, repeating the same faults.'

'When you seize the message of the Teacher, and the world of the spirit opens for you and you discover your own task, your destiny, you make a complete stop in your life, you do execute a psychic movement of 180 degrees, you turn your course in opposite direction, and trough the same path, the identical one you moved into your ruin, will also be your redemption, by this Way itself you do begin your return to the Home of the Father.'

'And you do observe, the constant suffering of so many lives lived in error, clearing immediately, and your Way becomes happy, joyful, luminous, as when Tom Thumb, gathers, on returning, the same small pebbles he applied in his descent.'

'It is then, when the professor, pricks his huge swollen mind, allows his spirit, his air, to return to the common wealth, and he becomes so insignificant, as Tom Thumb, he can only pay attention at the smallest incidents slipped back in his erroneous walk, and gathering those gadgets anew, rises joyfully to the Infinite.'

'And with this veer of 180 degrees you make a decision: I will be reborn one last time to carry out my mission in a perfect form.'

'Therefore Jesus said to Nicodemus:

- You have to be reborn, one more time, to enter the Kingdom of Heaven. If you are not reborn out of the spirit, you cannot live eternally in this reality.

'Then, you discover the Way and finish your reincarnations.'

'Jesus does not reincarnates any more, nor John the Baptist, either Manolo, or millions of souls that already followed the Teacher.'

'We are the residue, the only ones remaining on the surface of the planet, the remnants, the last ones, the lowest beings of our generation, the worse; still pawned in 'saving' our own individuality, without grasping to the words of the Teacher who said:

- Man will be redeemed only with Love.

THE GROUP

During more than seven years, a group of people gathered at Vilma's home to study the Bible.

From time to time we had visitors with new faces, so our meetings were always different, and many of them became sources of light.

I, for my part, learned a lot.

Yesterday we assemble again to study the 'Gospel of Judas' recently published.

We were considering a television program where the experts exposed their position on the subject, presenting a Gnostic point of view on Christianity.

After the video we reorganize the chairs for our discussion.

- To me, expresses Mari, all this is new. I never knew any of it, and it takes a lot to depart from what they taught me. Now in whom do I believe? Who were the Gnostics?

- The Way is different and unique for

each human being. You, Mari, head off from your pious education, and affirm your beliefs with the knowledge implanted in your mind by other people. You build your spiritual life on the understanding of someone else, on sand. Those individuals, for you, possessed the absolute truth, and you did accept them as such.

'Now, someone different shows you a point of view on Christianity completely opposed, the one of the enemy or the heretic, and such knowledge produces in your soul a disorientation. You don't know what to do or how to do it, and you find yourself confused and not discerning which path to walk.'

'Jesus spoke about this when He said; 'they will persecute you', it is not a physical harassment but psychic.'

'Unfortunate are the pregnant', He said, since you are fertilized with an embryo and still have not yet given birth to the Christ in you. This disconcert will continue more and more, and the only worthy of pity is you, because you see yourself conceived and at the mercy of thousands of ideas trying to ravage your maternity.'

'None of them cares for you. Neither your ancient instructors of the childhood, for whom you were one more number, nor the new experts, for whom you are an unsophisticated individual that has to be educated.'

'The easiest thing is to blame one or the other, but this position only avoids the solution.'

'What seems difficult is to recognize that you, with your inertia, have allowed yourself to be led towards destructive places.'

- And what do I do? Mari insists.

- Dear Mari, I cannot tell you what to do, because, if I scheme it, I place myself in the same tutorship of your ancient or new pedagogues, forcing you to walk through misplaced trails.

'It must be you, the one who searches for, in your heart, the source of water hiding within yourself. Do not search for it outside of you because it will make you shout:

- Already I am tired of following fake shepherds leading me but to the murrain and bitterness. I stay besieged eating food drawled to the hogs. I am in need of precisely raise myself from this predicament and return home to my Father, and tell Him:

- Father, I have sinned against the Heaven of my own destiny and have been hostile to You. I do no longer deserve to be called your daughter. Treat me as You do Your day laborers, but I want to be in Your House.

- The 'Gnostics', intervenes Rodrigo, presented a path of inside knowledge more certain than the one of conventional religion.

And, as if someone had opened the pot, I began with a long tiresome speech on ideas and concepts Gnostics have, showing the heretic viewpoint to the group.

For more than five minutes I spoke unceasingly.

- Where may I find Gnostic groups? Rodrigo asks again pulling me down from my ecstasy. I am reading a lot of on them, and learning great things. The only interest to me is to unite myself with God.

On saying this, the world of the heretics falls to the ground, breaking to pieces in thousands of useless excerpts, all my knowledge and eternal wanting,

I was telling Mari on the necessity of keeping ourselves independent, and at the same time I was falling into the hole of the opposition.

The intrusion of Rodrigo revealed to me the Truth.

- My beloved Rodrigo, I say, thanks for making me see the light on the Way.

'On one side it pulls me to institutional religion, on the other hand it drags me to the heretics, and the two factions, wanting me to be part of them, crucify me in their opposed logs, hauling me so strongly, they destroy my chest, dividing me in half, and my heart remains, alone, in the center.'

'Now I see the Way. So much force have they done against me, that they have destroyed me, leaving my head, useless and crowned with thorns, holding up aches and pains, but unable to produce fruit.'

'But the heart, they were not capable to steal it. And now I see it alone, abandoned, broken to pieces, in the middle of the Way, and sprouting in it a feeling indicating that it is in there, between the two extremes, that it has to be kept walking.'

'The solution is not to change factions, to shift from black to white, or from good to bad. The Way is to refuse the election, and to continue living, following through the tight path, that instead of trail it looks like a razor's edge. If you deviated a tiny bit, to one group or another, it splits and destroys you in two.'

'You are revealing me the essence of the Way: to keep ourselves in the midpoint position, advancing following the harmonic line between the two opposites.'

'The enemies, Pilate and Herod, allied to break the Messiah. The two factions, although appearing different, are equal, because they want you to be institutionalized, to get social power, to master the human heart.'

'And the two fail in their pledge, because no one is worried about your heart. They are wasting it, throwing it as null, relegating it to a harmful sentimentalism, pleased in their lowest carnal instincts.'

'At this time of enlightenment, I see two luminous beings coming together, the heretics seeds planted on the Spanish soil produce their best fruits, pointing for us the conclusion of our long meeting:

Saint Theresa of Jesus; fecundated with the qualifying 'of Jesus', indicates her fertility to the Teacher.'

- She is the reincarnation of Mary Magdalene, explains Vilma.

- And Saint John of the Cross, I continue, begotten 'of the Cross', deciding his total crucifixion.

'They teach us that in the Cross, in the center point, in the harmony of our Peace, we walk with God.'

'It is a useless Cross for the Gnostics searching for knowledge; absurd for those who look for political power and command. But for those who continue on the Way, in it we find the wisdom of God and the strength and the Divine acknowledgment.'

'This is the Christian Way.'

- Do not say 'Christian', repairs Elisa, because the path taught us by the Teacher is not a Christian trail. The shortcut He came to reveal to us, is a corridor for each human being, different, unique, amazingly great, manifested as a journey towards the human heart, towards peace and total freedom, it is the best and straightest approach to reach our Father. Name it simply 'The Way'.

WAI

- Come on, said the receptionist of the restaurant in Hong Kong, to Theo and me, when she notice us at the door.

The tiny place was jam-packed with small tables, one at the side of another, almost joining, inkling a popular dining room or common table. We were the only ones in the restaurant and she accommodated us in the corner.

After a few minutes she returned with a client, to whom she seated, almost in front of me, at the next small table.

He is a young worker from Hong Kong. He is dressed with an overall blue jean, big, clean and loose, indicating he works in an automobile garage.'

He had long and flowing hair, and he used it to isolate himself from others and he did not observe anything beyond himself.

He asked for a dish of spaghetti, without sauce. He ate it slowly and with difficulty, as he tried to cross the wall of hairs covering his face when bringing in each bite.

Our meal would go on like this, with the difficult position of been seated in front of somebody, that doesn't want even to go out beyond his hair.

After the supper we attempt to dialogue with him:

- What we sell, he says, it is what we do not want. If I desired something, or loved it, I would not sell it. What we handled to others it is what we abhor, the leftovers, what we despise, what is not useful to us. Therefore the capitalism is a waste, because it sells what it has to litter.

It puzzled me that this young man would speak in this manner, and much more when working as he was, at a car garage.

- Here in Hong Kong we sell it all, he continues, because we got more than enough. We are in want of nothing.

'We, the human beings, need nothing material to be fulfilled. Therefore money is the big lie. Having it or holding it not, for me, is the same thing. I run behind it, afterwards I gamble it all, lose it, and I return again to work to acquire more, to pay my debts, and again I return to play it and to dissipate it, in this routine killing all of us, and at the same time so necessary.'

- You look like a pessimist; I inserted

knowing that many Orientals are attracted to gambling and betting.

- You may, however, in this process, the youth continues without been bothered by my observation, acquire friends. The friendship is the only value for the human being.

The youth approaches the theme of friendship in an unforeseen form.

- Also for me, I pronounce. I know so many people, have so many friends around the whole world and I know they are my wealth. I am nothing at all without my friends, and friendship is the greatest treasure we may get in eternity.

'With them we work together in the constant pledge of growing, and we cross each others lives, once and again, loving or hating for the smallest thing.'

-Our evolution occurs in broods of human beings, Theo adds. Humanity is formed by small groups of people, having the same purpose for the common development.

'The beloved friend, therefore, is that one being we have selected before incarnating, at the beginning of time, the companion with whom we develop and with the one we are supposed to grow.'

- It is my opinion, I say, that in our different incarnations we know diverse human beings, and we integrate them to our small group, and this one increases and expands with new members; that, on being part of other groups, we link to each other in these threads of human history so surprising and affective.

'Each human being has a mission and a position in the general human history. There is no one missing, and not even one is a surplus.'

- But, everyone selects the friends he wants, Theo continues, and here it comes into action the freedom each one of us possess: divine gift, part of the essence, of the human light accompanying us, joyful guide dwelling with us for all eternity.

- But it is necessary that our mission be carry it out as a whole, the youth halts us in our chatter, and it is more a community goal than individual objective.

'My point, he continues, and I don't want to speculate with the idea of friendship, it is that, when knowing my friend, I accept all that he contributes to my experience: a being I allow into my life because his magnetism matches with mine; but, in his background, transports quantity of people, unknown to me.'

'When accepting him I give way to a crowd of individuals, indeed, to all humanity that he brings to my life.'

'Therefore, well sewed to our souls, we find quantity of relations, enhancing with time, and growing with us.'

'We all need each other, and when you accept someone else into your life, you let many specimens, the ones whom you also should help. And if you analyze each one of these units your friend supplies, you really manage to know all humanity, because each one of them, in turn, is embroiled to more and more entities.

'We all are in need of each other. Do love your friends, do not abandon any of them, on the contrary, hold them with your hand and walk together.'

'Tend your other hand to the remainder of the human beings, to the ones you owe nothing, because these are the ones who will return you in full one hundred per one, and will explain the hidden part of your friend.'

- May you comment on that? I pry.

- I have discovered that I am in this world to make a friend. And once I accept him as one, I receive, with him, all humanity.

'Some people opine that two is the number of the fight, and so we assume that the friend mutates into your enemy, and in this way of thinking we can not get out of the trap.'

'That is the reason why you don't understand what I announce.'

'I propose you a theme of conversation referring to friendship, and both of you place your efforts in lecturing me on a utopian lesson on acquaintances. You are slaughtering my idea.'

- Why? I ask.

- Because I am not referring to an idea, I am not addressing a philosophy, but pointing a reality.

'I don't search for a friend for having a companion. I search for a human being attracting me; and when accepting and knowing him, I discover this one being carrying in his heart a world, for me unknown.'

'His heart feigns it is all right, but it has a dark side, the dark side of the heart, and he has an atrocious fear to reveal it or to investigate its more secret corners.'

'And I, thinking myself attracted by the presence or the appearance of my friend, discover as the nucleus of attraction, not his external magnetism, but the dark side of his heart, he himself refusing.'

'And it is in there, when I begin to detect his dark intimacy that I find myself happy, because he reveals to me an unknown environment, offering me the gift of all humanity.'

'The dark side of his heart is the door of access to the Infinite.'

'I do qualify myself as a human being, to my friend as another: we are two. But he contributes to our friendship with his opaque side: a chasm so gloomy, somber and immense, that I call it, like the third sphere of our friendship.'

'This area is so independent and unique, that I estimate it like a third being in our relationship.'

'One of the many laws we have in our internal development is that we cannot self-analyze ourselves, we cannot get to see us in a mirror, because what we descry, is being perceived by our own eyes, therefore the self-observation is a crushing and absurd waste of time.'

'Our humanity has entered a channel of self-exploration taking us no place.'

'I have discovered this law: I cannot see myself, I need the support of another human being; and when I explore him, I inquiry myself. My friend is the instrument of my development. I need my ally in order that, helping him, I assist and discover myself.'

'If so, this third entity of which I speak, it is not formed only by the dark side of the heart of my buddy, but I, on deciding to explore it, intensify it with more strength, and graft in it the private and nocturnal place of my guts, and thread it with my being. In doing so, friendship is not of two, but of three.'

'All human development is an ascension with three people.'

'In this lower level rules the number two, but, when you move deeper in the study of the two, it is a third individuality what you discover.'

'And always, the true friend leads you to a third person.'

'To find the third is to uncover a third of reference, establishing the perfect equilibrium, the brilliant harmony, not with two notes, but with three.'

'Therefore I said before, the work is not private, but a common task.'

'Discovering a person, building my friendship, I reveal a dark connection to the Infinite, and when I analyze it the most, the better it presents itself and with determination it manifests.'

'I don't need to analyze myself: helping my friend reveals my own secret.'

- Have you seen those rings of three drop earrings? I ask.

- Yes, he responds.

- Once, I continue saying, I had an image of the human development, consisting in three circles, inserting into each other, soaring to the Infinite. Now, you have explained it to me, and I understand my perception.

- The table with three legs, says Theo, acquires the perfect rocking. The three strings plait it is difficult to break.

- In our development we all cross through capitalism, says the youth, turning over the conversation while still hiding behind his long hair; but we need to learn that it is in there to be exceeded.

'We gather to perceive that from the sky downwards, all of it is appearance.'

'The human being only needs light to evolve. Not a single material dowry is necessary for our labor. I give away all things material to achieve the intimate nakedness, helping my friend to penetrate in his dark heart, and in it, to discover Light. What more do we want from the future?

'Only when reaching the nakedness in the intimacy, he continues, we know of the need of friends.'

'I don't speak of removing clothes. That serves no purpose. Here we got public showers and baths and constantly we see nudity. But to remove your clothes is not to find the nakedness of the heart.'

'This one we acquire with personal development, when knowing ourselves, with that loosing of the knots of hate, dislike tiding us, covering each other with false masquerades, in enslavement relations.'

'The nakedness is to enter, without fear, in this dark heart and discover the Light.'

'And the Light is Love.'

'If you find a friend, and share Love, I am getting rid of the binds of hate, removing my past covers, letting loose of all material possessions, and finding friendship and freedom, coming together, and lasting eternally.'

'When finding a friend, you unearth Love, Freedom, Poverty, Happiness. You are in need of nothing material to acquire it.'

'Therefore I told you, at the beginning of our conversation, that money comes and goes, in a constant process and if we know how to use it, we may, in this capitalist and decadent society, craft eternal friends.'

The youth that ate a dish of pasta, without sauce, dry and simple, offered me a spiritual food of great quality.

- I also have my ideas regarding the Arts, he continues speaking. Art is a form of expressing the eternal feelings of our soul.

'But when the art turns into capitalist form, to export it, to sell it, this art of exportation, of commerce, turns out to be opposed to spirituality.'

'The gracefulness of Northern Europe sells tiny figurines with robust human forms. The stylized Lladro is fruit of a tough people. The elaborate forms of the Chinese art resists greatly with the simplicity of our spirit. The innocence of the Japanese art disagrees with his deep and complicated mental concepts. The French Impressionism is a consequence of a serene people. The Spanish abstract is the product of a concrete population.'

'The art of exportation, therefore, it is united to the economy. And the two are withered fruits of the mental appearance of the nations, in their complete opposition to their substance. Is not an Art born out of bravery, but an object of economy, and as a result, opposed and differed to its psychic effort.'

- I could not imagine, I tell him, that hair of yours concealing such penetrating eyes.

- The moral 'advance' of American export, he settles, is a result of a nation paralyzed in its Puritanism. The German stability indicates an unstable country. The Italian beauty is benefit of a rude earth. The Hindu clothes cover a population without marrow.

SIXTH CANTICLE

GETTING HIGH WITH WINE

THREE HUNDRED BOTTLES OF WINE FROM MY CELLAR

STEVE

- You are invited to use the VIP room, localized on the 12 floor. In there, they will serve you any wine or alcohol from 5:30pm until 8:30pm, and tomorrow breakfast from 6:30am, said the lady at the Reception Desk of the hotel in Denver, offering me, at the same time, the room key with a smile.

After dining, I decide to go to the VIP room and drink a glass of Cabernet.

The VIP room was a small area, with television and an affixed bar to the wall. Two seats in front of the bar, a sofa, and an office table, are the only pieces of furniture packing the area.

Two men, of about forty years old, were seated in the stools conversing with another individual, of about thirty years; with long chestnut hair combed in a ponytail. This last one did wear the uniform of the hotel, and he looked very clean, furthermore comparing him with the other two characters, sweated and dressed with blue jeans and T-shirts.

- Good evening. What do you want to drink? He asks me as soon as I enter the room.

- Cabernet, I indicate. He serves me a wineglass and I situate myself on the sofa in front of the television set.

The two men were looking for a plan for the remainder of the night, and with insinuations tried to find a weak part in the one offering them the drinks, but this one, with firmness and sympathy, evaded all of the insinuations, keeping himself in his position, with a lot of dignity, speaking in dialogue on the different topics of politics, literary and artistic presented to him.

His attitude did not portray any feminine manners of a manservant, or the stickiness of somebody hoping for a perk. His firm countenance, masculine, and with charm, shows an evolved soul.

The conversation is dilated for quite some time until, tired already in their useless labor, the two persons choose to withdraw to their rooms.

- Do you want another Cabernet? He questions me as soon as we remain alone.

- It is all right, I answer with a smile.

- Wow! He deposed, removing the sweat from his brow as a sign of alleviation, finally they left!

We remain for an instant without

knowing what to say.

- I observe that you are very well prepared on any topic of conversation, not only literary or political, but especially moral. I was listening to you, charmed, in the way in which you evaded any insinuation. I don't know if you will be offended by what I am telling you, I express, but it is not as a sign of insult, but as admiration: you appear to me like a Geisha.

- Ha, ha, ha, he laughs when listening to my comment.

- To me, I continue, the Geishas are instructed to serve, and they acquire the qualities I see in you. So be it, I am not telling it to you as a sign of affront, but as congratulation.

- I know it, he responds. The company I am working for sent me, without my willingness to do it, to Japan. There I learned the language and culture. As I was alone, I had lots of time for myself. I visited different places of the country, and at the end of the three years, I returned with my own theories.

- Hum? I muttered as a sign of answer.

- Japan is, for me, Steve says, the culture of serving. The servant is the opposite thing to the assistant. The aide is the one you give money in order that he supplies for your food, to massage your feet, to comb your hair. The opposite of the waiter is the servant. To him, you have nothing to offer, on the contrary, he gives it all to you for free.

'I, he continues, always have searched for happiness. In me, to be joyful is an absolute priority. And I found my bliss when I was in Japan. I saw it clearly, I had been designed to serve, and the more I served, the most ecstatic I was.'

'But it is not to serve in the hotel, offering dishes of food, or cleaning out shoes. It is a service that has nothing to do with that, it is an attitude, inside of me, of helping others to, through me, find that for them, and for all human beings, to serve, it is the base of the well-being.'

'I turn myself in a blade of rice, filled up with joy, somewhat fat and healthy, with an external smile, as Buddha, or somebody that has reached the nirvana, the perfection, and with each bow of my body, I invited also others to reach their zenith.'

'The servant, he explains, is the one preparing your Way, offering you the many intimate gifts he has, and his much intelligence, in order that you hasten in your search and may discover your prosperity.'

'The servant is the opposed thing to the helper. From the supporter you notice what he offers you, but from the servant, only with your Intuition, may discover what he is presenting to you.'

- What an interesting idea, I answer. But from what I have heard from you, it looks like you read a lot and know many things.

- I stare at a lot of books, he answers, but I know that books have no value. All of them are inventions, molded in words, fossilized and dead.

- And why do you read so much? I ask.

- Precisely, to serve others, to speak the same language and study the matching ideas, and from it, to lead them to the inside of their being, to themselves, so they may discover their joyfulness.

'I read and study to serve as an instrument to others, in order that they turn, as me, radiant.'

'But I keep myself outside from the others, without at least indicating to them what to do, and so keep my friendship.'

'Being friend, it is to serve; it is to offer others what you hold in your being. But you cannot tell them what to do or how to do it. Because as soon as you fall in this trick of the 'what' and 'how', this person becomes your enemy, because you are invading something private and nobody in the world has right to penetrate into the internal sanctuary that is the conscience of each human being.

'The search for happiness is supposed to be developed with innocence.'

'You presented me the concept of Geisha. She is a being that studies, reads, grooms, sing... a complete artist.'

'When evening comes, she covers her face with make up and dresses splendidly, to exhibit externally her internal qualities.'

'But what's going on?'

'Those observing her are only concerned for her wearing apparel, not for her essence or for who she is, but for what she represents.'

'And this is the root of enmity.'

'The one, who searches for you as a human being, finds a friend. The one, who wants you for what you simulate, or posses, or your social position, bumps into an enemy.'

'The will of another human being, because of envy or jealousy, yearns for what you tender externally, and covets to acquire it with force, violence and robbery.'

'The enemies are the fruit, not of the intimacy of your being, but of the immersion in the matter of a foreign will.'

'The antagonists in themselves are banal at the same time dangerous, and they envy your package, but not your contents.'

'Analyzing your enemy, you learn a lot, since he teaches you to value what you are, he discovers your intimacy, your superficial mistakes and the certainty of your actions.'

'Your adversary, when running over in his mind his own actions will be transformed into your friend. Thanks to him you maneuver better; compelling your will, he benefits from your conduct.'

'Only when you study your enemy, do you learn how much he teaches you.'

'When Jesus says: 'Love your enemy', he communicates a great Truth, because he is already your friend.'

- Are you talking to me about religion? I inquire.

- If you want to aboard that subject, we may converse on it, he responds without phobia.

- Let's face religion, I say.

- No, he clears up; we have been speaking of it the whole time.

- How?

- My experience is that they have strained it since childhood, he confesses.

'All those hours of Sunday study, memorizing Bible, demanding to feign, misfiring to go deeper into the essence, with a horrible pressure in your heart; so what, if you leave the home of your childhood, and you throw all of it to the dumpster, because every part of it, the whole of it, has been an absurd pressure from the outside, trying to manipulate you and coerce your will.'

'They have taught us external tactics, memorizing words without any content. We do dress elegantly to attend the functions; all of it is external conduct, without character.'

'The religious wear eye-catching, dazzling dresses, externally, therefore they yell for enemies.'

'As actors: all of it is appearance, and this form of wrapping up merchandise is what attracts the ones searching for what is public and not essence.'

'Consequently the professions of 'pretending': interpreters, religious, politicians, attract many enemies, people hating them because of their appearance in dress, or external beauty or power annexed to politics.'

'In this way all of them need a bodyguard to defend them. They do not care for their essence, since it cannot be stolen; they protect themselves because of the value of their possessions of wearing apparel.'

'In there you have precisely the base of the enmity. The same religious system, whatever its denomination, is based in dull and external premises, giving platform to the creation of enemies.'

- So do you have faith in nothing? I reverberate.

- On the contrary, I am revealing to you how to transcend the wrapping of the cult and investigate its essence. And when discovering it, you will find a friend, a being to love and to wait for.

'The religion is well placed as it sits, because you need to oppose the appearances and pierce into the intimacy of the geisha.'

'But along our lifespan, they assault many enemies, we do not need to create any more. I have to offer freely my service in the conscience, and don't bend to their desires, in order that everyone, through my joy, discovers the 'what' and the 'how' of his actions.'

'When I tell someone 'what' he has to do or 'how' he has to make it, worried only for his garments, I am grafting him with my will, wasting his conscience, and creating an enemy.'

'In order to have friends, avoid this intrusion.'

'True friendship is to accept others just as they are, searching for the warmth of their behavior, waiting for him to be sincere with you, without any coercion.'

'From where do they come from, these so called leaders, when their only thought is to impose their will on us and conduct us to depression?'

'I learn a lot serving. But when I found my joy, I discovered that everyone who is disciplining me, even my family, is saddening and killing me.'

'I discovered happiness in all of us, when we serve, and that joy obstructs gloom to penetrate into me and the despair of those who want to implant their will and be the powerful of the world.'

'This same felicity, gets me to be apart from 'the overbearing', because they confuse what is keen or helping with a servile attitude, and there is nothing as opposite as these two concepts.'

'That is why I remain employed in the hotel. Here the people comes to rest, as tourist or for business, but they arrive to find a little solace, and I find myself happy helping them; in this quietness, they obtain rest and everyone may utter what they carry in their inside.'

'Just imagine these two fellows looking for excitement. They kept trying to impose their will on mine, in the process, not to be my friends, but my enemies. If I would accept it and yielded to their aim, now I would be with them, sad, fulfilling their will, in a pleasure that neither is pleasing to neither me nor it has any purpose.'

'When avoiding their offer, not now, but possibly in some other time, if they still remember it, this one rejection will make them ask themselves 'why', and will offer to them a road of searching the intimacy of my being and my joy.'

'As soon as your enemies turn intelligent, they become your friends.'

- You have described with your words, I prompt, the fundamental essence of the Geisha. Thanks for sharing so much and going so deep. My intuition about you, opened my feeling, satisfying it with lots of happiness; something I didn't have for many years.

- Do you know that the better Geishas are males? He asks me asserting, while I was taking the elevator to go to my room.

LIN FAMILY

- Please sit wherever you want, said the tourist guide, indicating a sector of tables and seats.

- They will serve you a typical Bali meal, and you may, at the same time, enjoy the sunset behind the beautiful Temple.

The day of tourism was replete with visits to Sanctuaries and Oratories and most of the group, as me, sat down, exhausted.

In front of me accommodated a Singaporean family. The parents wanted to enjoy their holidays. Their daughter, a seventeen year old, remains absorbed in her shopping and daily souvenirs. The son, of twenty years of age, inquired constantly with his eyes, trying to penetrate into the essence of things.

- What is your opinion on Bali? The father asks me, filling with the conversation the tiredness of the day.

- It crushes me its overwhelming religion, I answer.

- Yes, he replies, the religion is a

necessity for a lot of people.

- Had you ever being in Singapore? He continues.

- Yes, I affirm tired.

- In there we have all religions, and every one of them is located in a sector of the city, and all the temples are filled with people.

'But I observe all those faithful and ask myself why they go to those buildings? What do they ask from their gods? What they offer them in return for their favors? What is the fruit of their religiousness?'

'As I do not see any result, I qualify all these religious forms as invalid, as they try to reach their gods with their tangible desires, refusing to approach their essence. The religious forms, show themselves distorted when we contemplate the purity of the Divinity, and compare it with the assembly of the pious.'

'All beliefs are coarse and deformed copies of the essence. Such high ideas of Karma and Reincarnation, when we see them materialized in the temples, become deformed.'

'When I enter a temple someone steals my energy, and I identify them as centers of darkness.'

The progenitor remains silent after his speech; his woman carries out a grimace of reflection leaning to her husband; the daughter continues absorbed in her gifts waiting for the drink that is taking a long time to arrive.

- The devotions are an appearance, asserts the son. That explains why properly it is called 'the opium of the people', because the religious groups are drugged by fictitious concepts, without possibility of giving them up. Neither they want to, nor can they search for anti-drug treatments, since they have no freedom of action, oppressed by banished forms, without any possibility of ending it. They grip the opinion of holding on to eternal ideas.

'Many great people arrive in our humanity, sharing their light with us. But the same humanity has made them gods, erecting temples in their honor. In this way they have expelled them as human beings, covering them with clothes. Have you noticed here how people dress even the images of stone?'

'They have covered these beings of Light with vestments externally attractive, with gold and precious stones, to make us believe that their ways were exclusive, so grand and difficult to go by, disconnecting them from the remainder of the population, from the normal people.'

'What they have done really is to

betray the initiator of the idea. And how much wrong they forge. With each temple, more gold, supplementary wearing apparels and the further we move apart from the Truth.'

- What are you doing? I ask him.

- I study psychology, the young man answers.

- It is curious that you present the subject of treachery in relationship to the religious situation of our humanity.

- When people search for your friend to betray you, the young man follows up in his saying; it is the worse wickedness that could be found on this earth.

'There is always pardon for your friend, but the work he has to do to deserve again your trust is extremely painful and difficult.'

'Those who plan the treason are different types of individuals, those working in the shadows, remain entangled in their snarl for a long time. As they don't oppose you openly but remain hidden, planning against your destiny with a wickedness directing them to the abyss, to the absence of light.'

'This weapon of the betrayal has been used by many people along the human history, but the scrupulous are the ones who have become experts on it.'

- My opinion is different; adds his mother.

- What do you mean? I ask.

- My paternal family is Japanese. For a long time their religion was intimately matched to the Emperor, and he was a god. The Americans arrive and do you know what?

- What? I ask.

- They removed their religion. When they saw their Emperor-god bow to a human being, their cult disappeared.

'And the same thing happened in different parts of Asia. Mao perpetrated it in the same China and Tibet.'

'We, Asians, are culturally ahead of the Westerners. You still have not a leader as impressive as Mao, who could display for you the uselessness of your devotions.'

- Are you advocating for violence? I investigate.

- Not at all, she responds. That one was the mistake of the Americans and of Mao. Intimidation solves nothing permanent. Therefore the cult resurges when the terror ends. And this is another annexed idea: there are people searching for fear as a technique to attain God. Many individuals match terror with dogma.'

'But I am referring to the development of the beliefs, without violence, not including fear, without terror.'

'What I perceive is a wall between the human being and the divinity. That divider is nothing else but the believers.'

'The so called 'holy men' try to approach the deity through the concepts of their founders. Do you think the fervent Buddhists represent the teachings of Buddha? How about the so-called 'Christians'?'

'I see them all like a farce, adorning the temples with gold, when Buddha, as Mohammed, Jesus and many others, discarded the opulence to live in poverty.'

- And a capitalist has affirmed these thoughts, I say smiling.

- That is the great American teaching, that we have to organize our society materially, but not mix our capitalist ideas with religion. Faith belongs to a world that everyone has to develop in their own style, avoiding to confront that wall of fanatics, and placing us near a God far above our low desires.

'And religious are we all when we believe that we must defend God.'

'God doesn't need anybody to safeguard Him, He helps Himself.'

The waitresses serve the drinks. The sunset dips with intense carmine dye the small Temple on the tiny island, permeating the reality with well-being.

- I wasn't hoping to hear such affirmations from an Asian woman, I manifest as soon as they serve our drinks. But your son, I say turning my head towards him, was communicating something on treason.

- What I wanted to express, he says, it is that, as there is treachery between us, there is also conspiracy against the philosophical ideas and the teachings of the great beings of light.

'The people call themselves 'followers' and they do exactly the opposite of what they suggested. And not only this, but, through history they have changed, little by little the original intention and, each year, with violent steps, they push the moral teachings towards the material chasm, betraying, with this, the spirit in which they were uttered.'

- You are revealing me something very deep, I say.

- The religiousness tires me a lot, he continues, and I think it is completely impossible to find Buddha, Mohammed or Jesus, asking the ones that classify themselves as their followers. Therefore Bali affects me not at all. The only object of my affection is to analyze the people.

- For me it is curious, I answer, that

you point the argument of treachery we commit against our Teachers, when we swap the original intention of their teachings.

- They come to help us, he says, but when we betray their teachings we are disloyal to ourselves. And when we disfigure their footprints, we wander prowling without direction or course.

- Do I understand you well, when you affirm that treason is the materialization of spirituality? I ask.

- I think so, he says.

The daughter remained isolated from the conversation.

- Is your drink pleasing? I ask her.

- It is all right, she answers.

- Do you have any idea in regards to what we are talking about? I pry in order to integrate her in the dialogue.

- My family, as you already have observed, does not harbor any religious practices. I visit the temples with my friends, and the Chinese sanctuaries attract me a lot, because when we enter them, slap twice, or we tinkle the bell, to wake up the gods.

'My friends and I enjoy asking them for a boyfriend.'

'When we finish the petition, we slap once or ring the bell, so the gods may turn to their sleep.'

'As they never respond, I imagine them not concerned about me.'

'I know there are monks, but rarely do I see them, and they do not attract me physically, therefore I do not worry about them.'

'The treason you are speaking of, for me, it exists, since none of these characters draws me: neither their thoughts, nor their ways.'

'But the concept of treachery is very important to me, especially at my age, and in school. Constantly we betray each other to embezzle our sweethearts or simply for the desire of making someone else suffer.'

'The traitor, truly, has to pay expensively the little pleasure she gets with her destruction.'

'What I did learn is that, to protect you against all this treachery, carry out whatever it is that you desire, but do not interfere in anybody's life. Take care of your body in health, cleaning, dress, and those things that will help you to center your life physically.'

'And asks fate to offer you the gift of another human body, in order that he or she may activate in you what is sleeping, and you may, loving another human being, know yourself and attain God.'

HANS AND RACHEL

Theo has contracted two painters, Rachel and Hans, to coat his house. When they finished the work he invited me. We all collaborated in preparing the meal, and we sat around the table to eat the last supper.

Hans is an engineer in computers, but, as he is not working in his trade, he paints.

His companion, Rachel, studied biology, and she wanted to specialize in the production of animals, but necessity made her change course, and now she also paints.

- Hans doesn't like to read, Rachel says as soon as we sit around the table, smiling merrily after uttering the phrase.

- I paid my studies selling books, Hans says.

- And how did you do it if you don't know what they contain? I ask.

- I offered thousands of copies of Herman Hess 'Der Steppenwolf', he responds. We had our monthly meeting, and they presented the book.

- What it is about? I questioned them.

- It is in reference to 'personal development', they answered.

- And I perceived, in the title page of the book, a wolf. Immediately I made up a story in my mind about personal development as it was to be alone in the forest, as this 'Steppenwolf'. And I taught it with such a conviction that I sold thousands of prints, but I never read it.

- It is curious, I say, because it is found in God's design that all people may develop and attain the mansions He has prepared for us in the spiritual ether.

'Well, I continue, this awakening has to be one by one, it is individual.'

'However, there are many beings around us, impeding these recollections. It is a necessity they keep this social appearance around us. They feed on this hate they embrace towards us and cheer on seeing us suffer.'

'When you feel sad, weak and depressed; when thinking that this world of the spirit is unreachable and unreal, you give base to these beings teeming around you, to describe the world that goes by roundabout you like a mirage of depraved cheer, of wealth that perishes, of love you cannot enjoy.'

'Therefore, we must gain strength in following the scent of our heart, sort out the depression of our mind, and attain the heart, digging out from it, the felicity awarding so much joy to your spirit and soul.'

'This is the Way of internal development: with your spirit, using the mind as an instrument, advance from the brain to the heart, open a trail of just one foot long, and move from the intellectual mirage and weariness, to the delight of your being.'

'In your feelings you will find the necessary elements for this wonderful alchemy of transformation.'

'In the daily happenings of yours and of those around you, you will localize the live jewels the Father sends to you at every moment.'

'Your Way it is to interchange them from the brain to the heart, and in there, transform them in your own treasure, discovering, gelds to geld, the external cover matched and glued to you along your terrestrial pilgrimage, and so find the innocence, the nothingness, the nakedness of the light.'

'In there you will become 'Der Steppenwolf', and in your loneliness you will find the light.'

'And in there you will perceive your

essence, that 'Sperma Logos', that small particle of the Word, which is Love. This is the material the Father used to create you, the same one which you need to mix with all of your experiences to become perfect, to be as our Father. And, would that you may return to the place from which you went out and present yourself in front of Him without any cover.'

'You will be then, as He, creator. And you will work with Him creating and loving more and more, for all the eternity, reaching to new skies and new earths.'

'This is the road of Calvary, in which you won't suffer any destruction, because then, and only then, the vision becomes so real and clear, that forms in the spirit, a constant obsession to walk towards the Light.'

Truly it appeared to be the last supper and I follow with my long tiresome speech of endless ideas that had no repercussion in them.

- For me, nothing of what you say means a thing, he shorts cuts me. I don't read, and if you present to me a discussion on religion, it repulses me so much, that I block myself from it.

- Let's change subjects; says Theo.

- Not! I shout, it is of interest to me.

- Let's drink a toast with red wine in

order that our hearts may harmonize and we may bring out the Truth in our gathering, exclaimed Theo. serving wine at the same time that he said it.

- He has read only a book, says Rachel, and it is from that one scientist, I never remember his name, the one of the black holes.

- Ah! Hans comments. That is a good conversation. That is truly a Book, when analyzing the universe, we scrutinize our society, and so I am going to reveal you what I feel.

'In the universe there is a center of attraction, and in certain form it magnetizes heavenly bodies next to it, and concentrates them. But this one nucleus, in order to move, has to have certain opposition. Therefore, as soon as a nucleus magnetizes itself, it has to create enemies, in order that the opposing force could generate the energy of the movement. Consequently the hate is the motor of the universe. For that reason, we need to have enemies and be betrayed, so to move, because without them we would be stuck together in the center, without any possibility of evolution. The hate, the enemies, is the perfect gift to maneuver.

- My grandfathers were German Jewish, it utters Rachel, and my grandmother told me the story that when they got out of Germany and moved here, they did not want to know anything of Jews nor of their religion. She informed me that her world was destroyed completely.

'My grandmother was clairvoyant, and she said of Moses, formed himself in the wisdom of the Egyptians, when instituting his religion and in order that this one could get strength and move, he placed the Arabs as his enemies. So be it, my grandmother has already known about the centers of attraction.'

- The interesting thing in this, continues Hans without paying attention to Rachel's intervention, it is that these centers, when moving, make it in form of whirlwind, a spiral, magnetizing towards its depth, all the energy of the bodies joining them.

'And there begins the interesting thing.'

'These communities present themselves attractive, in order that the objects without their own essence befall fascinated for what they offer, and stuck together with one of them. And once they plunge into the trap, the movement of slow intensifies more and more, the deeper they drop.'

'The one located at the bottom, the

leader, it is the one who has more, because all of this energy is concentrated in only one nucleus. But it reaches a dot, in which the same force of concentration is so powerful, that exploits, and when blasting it expands those millions of bodies, returning them to the borders of the universe, in order they may continue, again, their evolution.'

'That expansion only pertains to the substance. Here on the earth it cannot be executed, because, just imagine how interesting, the water sticks together all the terrestrial elements and does not allow their escape evasion. The water is the fixation of the matter on this earth, and it is an element that forces us to come down from our height and to concrete in what it is physical.'

With this, Hans explains to me, in a cosmic way, without perceiving it, the history of my soul.

And in front of me I noticed a philosophical tendency, attracting towards itself, millions of peoples without quality of their own, going down with each circumvallation, towards a center of power, and so to be smashed and to suffer defeat.

- But these two opposed whirlwinds, Hans continues explaining, are always rubbing. Just imagine those who call themselves Christians: they have created the heretics, so they may maneuver: they are their eternal enemies.

- Do not speak to me of anything on this subject! I am already tired of so much! Theo says.

- That it is where I want to go, continues Hans without any concern. These heretics criticize the institution because it has not behaved correctly. But these Gnostics, or Heretics, or Freemasons, being in power today, still make it worse.

'Just imagine in South America: all these nations, for centuries, doing nothing. San Martin in Argentina, Bolivar in Venezuela, they were Freemasons, and did not achieved to help the great, needy, native people. Their circle is smaller than that of those so called Christians, they have more power, and in the whole planet each time they do it worse, and they still criticize the inquisition, when they don't know where to go: they only accumulate money.'

'And there are not two groups only. In the whole planet there are thousands and thousands, in constant friction, one against the other. And what is curious is that all of them act the same. It is like the stock market, it absorbs more and more money, and it reaches to a point, where it self-explodes and falls, drawing pitilessly the forgetfulness its thousands of investors... and after wasting them, begins again to attract others who are not cautious that fall into the trap, to continue the same process.'

'The solution is not to know which one of these circles is the best, what you need to find is the way of not falling into their trap'.

And then, appears in front of me, the image of the Way.

The Way is this point of friction, between two opposing whirlwinds. The travel is to emanate harmony between these two dissonant sets, it is in balancing the opposed forces, it is found sliding through the tight and destructive edge, avoiding falling into one of them.

Hans clears in lucid concepts my subjective ideas.

- Another concept emanating from here is that, when you want to materialize your ideals, you kill your dreams of evolution.

- This physical world, it inserts Rachel, is a blue copy of the psychic, but it is an inverted reproduction. So, the Egyptian Pyramid is a distorted tracing of the original. The peak of which will not take you to the stars, but to the depth of the planet.

- These black holes, Hans sharpen his opinion, are cycles. When you enter into one of them you stay in the cycle, outside of them the Time ends.

- And when you invert the vital thing over the solid, adds Rachel, the Space disappears.

- The speed of attraction in the black holes, presses Hans, is faster than the speed of the light.

- These bodies of attraction, introduces Rachel, have to feign attractive, to draw more entities. This seduction gives more energy to the organism.

- The one who has more, prompts Hans, descends the most, because the extra you possess, the less you want to lose your wealth, this being your force.

- It is like the magnet, clarifies Rachel, you do have to remove your whole metal, in order that the attraction will not draw you, and you may get free.

- The liberation, or redemption, spurts Hans foreseeing the sublimity, it is question of a second, and it is extremely short. But you cannot be in the matter; you have to live in the pure spirit.

Hans and Rachel courted in unison. They represented for me the perfect marriage, the opposition so contradictory and certain of the antagonism, where degradation doesn't flow, but independence springs up.

- But this is increasingly interesting,

continues Hans, since these two opposing circles move in perfect balance against a third entity, as the black hole.

'This black hole, really, is the only beginning, from which sprouted out the other two organisms. But these two opposing corporations, to relegate more, don't speak of it, for them, the third modulate unit doesn't exist'

- That is what my grandmother tried to say, Rachel stops us. Moses learned it from the Egyptians, and established his religion with enemies. The two of them fought without any concern towards Egypt, from where they went out. And Egypt attracts them magnetically, until the two of them finish by squandering, mutually absorbed by the same nucleus from where they came from. Therefore, when my grandmother perceived this reality, she lived isolated from the scent of any foreign magnet, and she remained, ignoring all of it, harmonizing her life, and loving the Arabs more than those of her own race.

- In their progress, Hans continues, keeping up in his level, remiss to the interferences of Rachel, these two whirlwinds are attracted towards this center of obscurity which has more strength than they do, and causes their mutual friction, at the same time awaiting, until they collide against each other, to trigger the explosion of these bodies and absorb in it, all of the matter, disseminating it to the borders of the universe.

- Do you know that all religions have gone out of Egypt? Even the Catholic one, affirms Rachel developing her idea with the indications of Hans; and the Pope does not looks like a Caesar but as a Pharaoh.

- This black hole, it is the door to another universe, persists Hans

- This is wonderful, I comment.

I find myself trying to find a balance between the two conversations, harmonizing in two whirlwinds of friction.

The dialogue is divided in two levels, antagonistic among themselves. And like all eternal truth, reverberates until the most tiny particles of the planet, when listening to the dissonant unison, they manifested to me the perfect marriage.

Moses, when instituting the marriage forces an enemy in your home, which promotes your energy and eagerness of development. The children would be, then, this black hole, point of attraction, destruction and regeneration of both.

- And this also applies to the gods, renews Hans. The god creating this world, with its opposed spheres and with its black holes, has a superior god, and so, endlessly, until reaching the God Almighty or Highest, as He is called.

'Have you questioned anytime where the idea appears of having only one language, only one government? This proposal of material unity, insists Hans, is a Utopia worse than any other. Because there are thousands of circles, that successively burst; and the diversity, the opposed, the enemy, are necessary in this lower world, in order that this sphere may move and progress.'

'This planet is like a ball filled with holes, ends Hans. Between them you must find your passage, eluding them and without allowing yourself to be trapped by them.'

- And if you do fall into one, finishes Rachel, you must get out of it. But you do not even need or gain courage to do it, because in each one of these circles there is a hidden force that expels the undesirable persons.

- Stop your philosophy, sticks Theo, and prepare the dessert and coffee and listen to the Word of the Teacher, when it says:

- Truly I say to you, they will expel you and, with this, they will give glory to God. I am telling it to you before it happens, so that when it occurs, you may know that I had already said it.

SEVENTH CANTICLE

THE SONG OF SONGS

THREE THOUSAND MELODIES

BANGKOG

GUY

- Are you staying in Hong Kong? The passenger seated at my side, Guy, asked me a few minutes before the airplane landed in Hong Kong.

- Not, I indicate, I am going to Bangkok.

- Is this your first time in Hong Kong? He insists.

- No, I prompt, truly I really do not count them, because I got this ticket to visit a few cities in Asia, and I must connect always through Hong Kong.

- I travel a lot to Asia, affirms Guy. It enchants me. Always, there where I go, I do glimpse the hands. With time I have formed a theory.

'When I enter America, I realize the Americans have no hands. When coming through customs, with his eyes they ask you to open your luggage, and during the inspection they treat you as if you were polluted, evading the personal touch.'

'In Canada, where I am from, it is still worse, they avoid all physical contact and they ask you to show them what you carry on, but they don't even deign to touch you. They treat the Asians so poorly...

- Do not remind me, I expose, because after the last time, when I reached Vancouver, they asked me endless questions, for hours, doing photocopies and a quantity of absurdities, that I made the decision not to return.

'And not only to me, but they treat almost all visitors wrongly, specially the Asians.'

- Precisely I am from there, he responds. But when you reach the Orient you discover people with hands. The Japanese use their detectors in an imperceptible form.

'The Chinese want to touch you, and they have an extremely pleasant touch.'

'I position the Koreans between Japanese and Chinese, appealing to both contacts. But they use specially the eyes to find out about you.'

'The Thai caress you smoothly...'

Guy went through, one by one, all the Asian countries he knows and values.

- But where I find the perfection of

the planet is in Hong Kong. The immigration agents, women and men, are so young and beautiful, that I aim to be touched by them whenever I come to Asia. But they scarcely grub my clothes, the touch is so perfect and imperceptible, that it reaches my soul.'

He sketches a smile of placidness to assent his philosophy.

- The Europeans do not even want to touch you, they allow you in or out like another number of visitor. The Asians are the only ones with hands and using them, although their touch is not visible, but intangible.

The airplane landed and I did verify Guy's philosophy in all its glory.

The idea of the touch, however, accompanied me along the following days.

THE GUIDE

A few hours later I took a plane to Bangkok, the city of Angels. I was three days in Thailand.

The first day we visited the Imperial Palace, with its famous golden temples and the impressive paintings, hundreds of meters long, describing the Mahabharata epic poetry. It represents in it the spiritual history of the Ancient Vedas.

The guide explains about a 'being' appearing once as angel and later as demon. I importuned him with so many endless questions, until, weary, he answered me:

- That is the root of the problem of division untaken between the East and the West. You catalog a person as good or bad, condemning him forever or redeeming him for all eternity. And that, for me, is an error.

'We Asians know that good and evil are a fraction in each one of us, the Yin and Yang, the white and black, the positive and negative: the division is in us.'

'It depends of our own actions, if we

work well we move towards the light, if we conduct ourselves with wickedness, we waste ourselves.'

'The Angel and the Demon are in me. Drift of my will that I bring it forth in one way or another.'

This idea breaks up the mirage of my western mind.

In the West we catalog some one as an 'Angel' and we predestine him to be a perfect individual; and if he commits any error, we pardon him immediately because he works against his essence, that is immaculate.

On inverted manner, when we qualify a subject as a 'Demon', although he may do as much good as possible, we sanction him forever.

The guide, without even touching me, broke to pieces my mental hallucination, exposing the essence of each human being.

SUNAN

After visiting the floating market, immediately after lunch, we stopped in Phra Pathom Chedi, the most important temple of Thailand.

- You've got an hour and a half to take a walk and enjoy the Temple, the guide said, with desire, himself, of resting and finding a little solace in his work.

I went towards the temple. At the right part of the entrance, a monk was seated in the position of lotus, in dialogue with a married couple.

I remain observing him for quite some time, with his saffron tunic, his serene face as of a Buddha, in an attitude of perfect harmony, subjugating me so much.

After few minutes the pair stands up, offers him a gift rolled in plastic, bowed reverently in front of the young monk, and withdrew from the place.

In the opposed side of the door, I found a step and took a seat. As I wanted to converse with the monk, but did not know the language, an idea occurred to me: I am going to relax and try to contact him spiritually.

I quieted myself for a few minutes, balanced my full stomach, I entered my inside peace, and asked permission from the monk:

- May I seat in front of you and interchange ideas? I asked in my intimacy.

I opened my eyes, turning my head towards the monk, and I discovered him watching me.

I smiled and closed my eyes. Already I knew he was listening to me, I had connected and we were in tune.

- I also am a monk, but of a different religion, I say, I go searching, in each excerpt of the world, for what people may tell me about God. And today, casually, I am in front of you. I could not discern if this is the first time that we find each other in our respective incarnations, or we already know each other from the past and this is a new awakening. I do want to embrace and rediscover you but I cannot even move. We are like two sentries at the side of the door, receiving with love all those who cross it and I ask God to give you energy to continue in your walk so you may arrive quickly at your destination.

- In a few days I will leave from here,

he responds. I offered five years to the Temple; I have studied a lot and prayed frequently searching for my ascension in my quietness. The days here go by contrary to my original intention. The superiors stop me here at the door, to receive the faithful and to advise them in their problems.

- May you comment something on your spiritual development? I investigate.

- I am a pacifist and Peace is my delight. The government offers us the opportunity, in our youth, of choosing, between the military service and the religion. And I selected the religion.

'Since childhood I am attracted by the ideas of Buddha. Therefore, to enter into a temple, to study and to reach perfection was my puerile desire.'

- Truly, I voice to accent his narration, it is an image, also for me, supremely attractive, the one of a youth with saffron tunic. That's why I am here, fascinated by you.

- I, besides the time stipulated by the government, decided to lengthen it a few years more, and possibly extend it for the remainder of my days.

'At the beginning it was all right, with the study, the physical work, the meditation, the help to others.'

'But afterwards, on graduating, they

place me as counselor, assigning me a seat in the temple, with a schedule and norms of external conduct. And what was a desire of perfection; turn out to be a jail I cannot evade.'

'Without my own perception, they used my idealistic immature tendencies to enslave me into a building.'

'I am so fixed, stuck together to this one door, that already I believe my entrance into the spiritual temple is impossible.'

'Buddha taught a road of perfection removing our desires. In youth, sex is the major appetite, and I dedicated myself constantly to purity. But, the most chaste I was, more intensely I caused cravings on others, and the young ladies came to me constantly, inventing fictitious problems, to be near me, desiring me.'

'With time I earned trust in myself, and certainty in the Buddhist way of perfection through purity and chastity.'

'But this honesty and cleanness is found in our spirit, and we may keep it, even while married.'

'Kundalini, the internal snake, sleeps in the coccyx, next to the sexual organs. When waking up it finds two hallucinations: reaching God trough channeling religion or guttering sex. Most of the humans follow the obfuscation of the genitals, others, those of the religious ambitions. But Kundalini has to walk through these two tendencies.'

'I have achieved to discover that the snake advances not as part of the 'general population' and not as branch of the temple. She is despised, inconsiderate towards, defamed by the two prejudices, obsessions, blindness; but Kundalini drains until reaching Nirvana. She is the Truth.'

'And what it is the temple and the sex, but the same thing? One only desire of dominion over you, when crushing Kundalini's mind.'

'The two forces attempt to be against your freedom and joy.'

'But you do not understand me, he continues resigned. You accept what I am telling you as a teaching, a theory, something as utopia. And it is not so.'

'If you want to advance in the spirit and ask your mind, she offers you what she perceives, and what she distinguishes are these two streams: religion and sex.'

'I have told you they are two fictitious torrents, because the people moving by sexual impulses invent a quantity of absurdities to make themselves secure in their point of view, and believe themselves to be owners of the truth.'

'They promote, therefore, their idea of sexuality and procreation to the extreme of taking it beyond the grave.'

'The religious flow devise theories related to sexual purity and chastity, ideas that we could not find in the flesh. When in finding themselves impotent to curb these impulses, they cover themselves with wearing apparel of beautiful colors, in order that people stick themselves more to what is exterior unconsciously, than to what it is the dress of our human skin.'

'The devout avoid the study of the human nature, because perceive it as impure and unworthy of inheriting a spiritual reality.'

'The sexual, penetrate on treaties of genital organs by searching for the origin of life. As it cannot be found in the flesh, they conceive a quantity of fictitious concepts trying to prove they are in certainty.'

'Both of them are in complete error because they avoid the study of the human being.'

'We are not sexual or asexual. We are Beings. We Are. Complete. Unique.'

'If you want to evolve intimately, start analyzing what you hold within the reach of your hand, your human body. And do not look at it as sexual. Who has told you such error? Do not either peek at it as asexual. Who has proposed to you a similar fault?

'Do analyze each cell of your body. Each one of them has its individual function. Also there is a part in them enclosing a collective task, because they are integrated to a life organism.'

'The sex exists in the human creature. But sex is not the genital limb. All the cells of the body are part of this sexual life form. Have you perceived that each cell thinks, reflects and feels, it has memory to feel every single one of its experiences? How do you dare to fraction your corporal understanding into a single sexual organ? Such little love you have towards yourself, to practice daily a single extremity, abusing it until the extreme, without giving it a moment of rest? What absence of love towards yourself, and of injustice, when you use a fraction on you body with contempt and hate, locating it pejorative in relation to the others.'

'The religious act oppositely. They cover their genitals and conceive the idea of the asexuality in God. Their concepts turn in their gods. And the mind is their only god.'

'Kundalini, the snake, the one I am speaking of, is not easy to be found. In fact, she doesn't exist physically in the organism.'

'But when you study each one of your cells, and you love them, it appears, in front of your spiritual sight, a psychic force keeping them together.'

'This ethereal figure, little by little it concretizes in the shape of a snake. And Kundalini is the vital force, completely invisible in the flesh, but feeding itself on each one of your cells.'

'She teaches you to treat equally all parts of your body, or in other words: she indicates that you must remove your organs from the control of the mind, in order that they may develop with the foreseen design of the Creator.'

'With Kundalini you learn to withdraw your mind from each organ and to fill it up with love: a substance extremely expensive and healthy.'

'Kundalini always is threatened by the religious and by the sexual people because both of them want to ensnare it for their own end of power and control. But she moves between them, intentionally being not a fragment of any.'

'The one, who finds her, obtains freedom, purity and chastity. Therefore I have said you she is the Truth.'

'The Truth is that internal and spiritual way, oppressed by the two extremes. It is a weak thread, serpentine and imperceptible, leading us to perfection.'

'How happy I am in my life, when I go alone to the river. I remove all of the vestments and plunge into the water. There I discover myself as a perfect Being, finding peace in each one of the cells of my body, showing a way that it is Truth and Life, confirmed as health, purity and humility.'

'Therefore, when I do fulfill my commitment, I will get out from this door, that has not been prearranged to me by God, but by enslavement powers.'

'Your initial words are authentic. For an instant, 'we have been two sentries, without heads, at the side of the door, receiving with Love all those who cross it'.'

'The essence of Kundalini is Love, the mighty stream passing through between the physical and ethereal worlds.'

'The Almighty, with your presence, has established my internal energy, in order that I may continue advancing and may reach my destination.'

KLAHAN

After dining, the tour guide took us to a cabaret, where a group of female impersonators maintain a show.

Some Asians, especially in Thailand, when they are young, have the skin and features so feminine, which can feign women.

The managers, to promote the local industry, organize shows with these young people, trying to please the tourists and have some fun.

They offered a drink, I asked for a beer, loafing at easy to observe the performance.

During the program, and with humorous intention, they removed the top of the dress of their companions, letting everybody see they were not females, but males.

The joke was not funny to me, producing some kind of seduction because of their physical form, at the same time as repellent, for their psychic character.

The hermaphrodite form was the conducting root during the Renascence, and the artists searched to mold individuals in their work, holding these two qualities.

But when I saw them dressed as women and joking about the subject, I felt isolated from the show.

Observing the benefits of a few hours earlier, I reflected in my innermost self, I would like to practice the same system I used previously with Sunam. From between all these youths, I selected one of them, and tried to communicate internally with him, so he could indicate me his notion of God.

Whom I select? I asked myself. Those on the front rank did not appeal to me, but I perceived a youth, almost hiding in the third row of actors. His penetrating eyes were observing a world beyond the theater, and interpreted the program without contentment.

- What do you think about Life? I ask him in my inside.

- I don't conceive anything, he responds. The Life is.

'It is manifested in us in two forms: the woman, like a flower asking to be observed, caressed and penetrated; and the man, perceiving, kissing and guessing.'

'But neither of these two influences is energetic, they are deviations of Life itself: a fiber flowing exactly between the two, but not a fraction of them.'

'The masculine and feminine elements try to create a new life, but what they reproduce is a being, already living by itself before sprouting. These two vital forces cannot grub the life flowing between them both.'

'To understand what Life is, you do have to pour forth between these two opposed poles, between the woman and the man, and become a hermaphrodite.'

- Ha! I laughed abruptly, but I curbed it immediately, so as not to laugh at the idea or to be discourteous with the youth.

- Are you laughing? He questions. God is not man or woman. God creates the human being to His image, and forms two opposed bodies: the male and the female. But God is neither a guy nor a spouse: He is androgynous.'

'He has a unique and different form, not molded sexually.'

'Do you understand me? He shouts at me, he is not half one and half other: He is completely different.'

'That one is the problem of those who have identity crisis. They got such a lack of brains. If they are male, remove their genital organs to be exchanged for a female. And they will never be women because, in our world, we cannot mold the idea of hermaphrodite.'

'What they only get is not to change their sex, the sex is not switched over, but to drop the energy they had, and be transformed into an asexual being, which is completely opposite to God.'

'God is not the one who has lost his procreating quality. He is pure Life. He is not in need of anything different to keep Himself alive. He exists carrying the two traits of the male and the female, not wasting them, but grafting them as part of His being.'

'On the other hand, God begets life in Him, not outside Himself. He is an internal and not public creation.'

'The one who modifies his own genital organs is discarding the gift of Life, for an absurd idea of changing sex.'

'The solution, not only for them, but for the whole world, it is keep ourselves hermaphrodites, walking through that tight line, being despised, so much for the males as for the females. Your concept of perfection and of Life, is found in the middle of these two fractions; but it is uncovered as a unique estate, detached and relegated, being the essence of the divine Life.'

'Then, when you advance through

this Way, not needed and discarded, you localize chastity and purity. They have rejected you from both sexual dots and you become, not asexual, but the conflicting opposite entity: a pure and chaste being with beautiful genital organs.'

'The sex is divine grant, but you, like the remainder of the people, accept it like a curse, and afterwards, as with a minimal attitude, still want to analyze the donation God bestowed upon other beings; and you try it, for seeing if it is better or worse than the one you hold; and so you remain always on the surface of the cover unintentionally wanting to open it and discovering the spirit transcending it.'

'You all are blind, and encourage yourselves in your blindness as you do not search for the essence of the Being.'

'Be brave, and decide to integrate yourself in this intermediate way.'

'But take it as an inner decision. And do not prove it to anyone. Life is an inside and intangible, pure and chaste strength that doesn't want to be touched nor abused, but caressed, subtly, with love.'

'Love is not found, therefore, in sex. Is not a fruit of the carnal bond.'

'I don't become man or woman as I dress myself as either of them. The costume covers our nakedness. The spectators are attracted by the appearance externally, but they never perceive my Being.'

'And on the other hand, nobody will accept me for who I am, because they all refuse my essence. They are all condemned to senselessness by enjoying only what is the façade of my being.'

'And I find myself in an intermediate attitude. And this third condition is the essence. What I am trying to say is: I keep myself on my path, renouncing the appearances and localizing the Being of Life.'

'In the exterior forms we look like sexual. In the marrow we may find Love.'

'And Love causes Humor. The Humor sprouts in you when you see all of the people feigning a sexual knowledge, and what they only show, seen from the stage, are their lower desires of sexual control and of their sick mind.'

'If you do accept sex as divine alms, you are not to become a judge of the desire of others, neither to make fun of somebody else's feelings, knowing neither their past nor their future.'

'When you do not pass judgment on others you begin to perceive this gift like a charity, in which chastity promotes Love and Humor.'

'And it is a contagious humor when

you discover the trick of the human appearances. A felicity sitting happily in the intuition of your heart, to attain the two energies of eternal aid: Humor to discover the essence and make fun of the appearances; and Love to share your vital organs, not your body, with the loved ones.'

'In here is born the purity and chastity, because to be hermaphrodite is an idea not molded in the flesh. In our tissue we are well shaped between male and female. To be androgynous is to untie ourselves from the flesh, and knowing us as sexual, direct our efforts towards the spirit.'

'It is then you become an Angel and live in Bangkok, the city of Angels.'

SYDNEY

KATHY

- Welcome to the Aboriginal Cultural Center, says a young, very attractive blond girl, as soon as she perceives us entering the quarters.
- Thanks, I answer.
- Is this the first time in Australia? She investigates.
- Yes.
- What do you think? She inspects.
- I am, after walking throughout Asia, not in Paradise, but in the Heavenly Jerusalem, because I don't find any temples.
- We have them, she remarks.
- But compared with the whole of Bali, I do not perceive any.
- All right, welcome to Australia. My name is Kathy, and I am a volunteer here in this Cultural Center. Australia is a continent in many ways different to others, unique, extremely beautiful, but what we have best

is the people.

- That explains it; I said as to fix her words. In here, I am much better off than in paradise, I have attained the Heavenly Jerusalem, the highest perfection that could be achieved on this planet.

- We have a program of Aboriginal Culture in forty-five minutes, she explains without any consideration towards my observation.

- It is fine, I answer. Now we take a walk around here, and in half an hour we will return to attend the program.

- Do you know something about painting? Kathy questions.

- I like it a lot, I answer.

- Do you want to visit our painting collection? She proposes.

- Yes, I reply.

Immediately Kathy leads us to a door and opens it, the inside is dark.

- Do enter! She points with her hand in order that I penetrate in the somber area.

- What a marvel! I exclaim, when, in lighting the hall, falls over me a quantity and a variety extremely wonderful of colors and forms.

- Do you know something about Aboriginal painting?

- Nothing at all, I answer. However, it has a powerful attraction over me, and I cannot explain why it pleases me so much.

- The Aboriginal painting, explains Kathy, is different from all other canvas. Your painters sketch peoples, clothes, faces, colors or landscapes. Even in the abstract art, or Picasso, there are personalities in the flesh, landscapes or objects that are material: all the drawing is matter.

'The Aboriginal skill is a spiritual technique. In each work of art they describe their walking in the spirit.'

- How? I ask with curiosity.

- Do you see these dots? Each stitch represents a step in their spiritual hike. This crushing continuity of incrustations means each footstep in their constant movement.

- Just look at this cane in the form of an 'I'.

- Ah! I exclaim.

- It represents a male, with the twig of the penis. The "U" stands for the woman, with the womb. Here we got two canes, indicating she encountered two males; a little farther there are two 'U', showing two women.

- This is extremely interesting, I manifest enthused.

- Look the animals, continues Kathy. Don't they appear different to you?

I observe the silhouette of the reptiles filled with lines.

- It is because they are clairvoyant, clarifies Kathy. They observe the world of the spirit constantly immersed in matter, and when they paint in their spiritual pilgrimage their encounter with other people, they describe them only as sexual individuals; and they represent the animals with their internal and nervous organs.

- Do you mean to say, I ask, that the Aboriginal clairvoyant see in us, humans, only sex, and the animals surpass us because they possess members and nerves, besides their sexuality?

- I don't go as far as to say-so that they eclipse us, continues the guide; but yes, they revere them as beings helping us on our spiritual walk, and with which we share our earth.

Kathy directed us, from painting to canvas, showing a variety of minute and countless dots, in this spiritual path. Each pilgrim treasures his color. Each step is perfectly delimited, neither without mixture nor with the precedent or the following. Each advance is exclusive. And the hallway straightened up all covered with small points, without touching, representing the ache and the joy of the human terrestrial pilgrimage.

And as, many years before, in Hawaii, when my ears opened to a psychic music, on the other side of the Pacific Ocean, my eyes burst with an explosion of the color of the spirit.

And my joy intensifies so much that I begin to weep of emotion. My eyes are cracked to the light, and in front of them cross millions of people, divine pilgrims, finding other living individuals.

- My dear brother Michelangelo, I exclaim to my innermost self, wherever you may be, you have to come to Australia to start painting, not the Sistine Chapel, but our everlasting pilgrimage towards the Light. Do use the multicolored sand and spread it, in your walking, throughout this continent, retelling our eternal whereabouts. And allow the wind to liven up your images and bring together our steps with those of all the humanity, painting on the tapestry of the earth, the colored multiplicity of the human race. Look what a beauty! Observe how much tint! This is pure Impressionism! None of any colored dot dissolves with another, there is not physical mixture. In our pace we find colored diversity, but each one is individual and unique. But when we perceive them with the eyes of the soul, all this variety becomes One and with millions of colors we glimpse the Light.

- Thanks a lot, Kathy, I say sobbingly, for opening my eyes to the Light.

- Good! She answers, thanks to you for coming, and for allowing me to instruct you in my culture.

JEREMY

- My name is Jeremy! A young man said, introducing himself from the stage.

I felt so moved by the teaching of Kathy, that I was grateful for the darkness of the theater and the anonymity among the group of people attending the show.

The act included only one artist, and it was Jeremy.

He explained his family to be, in part, Italian. As a child, he was sent to live with his aboriginal grandparents, and in there, he learned all of what he knows.

- The Aboriginals have a practice and it is that when we are fourteen years old, they send us to discover our Way.

'The father, in my case my grandfather, calls his son and directs him, empty handled, so he may find his Way, and afterwards, in his return, he must communicate all of what he perceived.'

'So be it, I am already giving you the first word we learn in our culture: to observe.'

'All our human whereabouts are spots to watch, to discover, to reveal or to sing.'

'They sent me, alone, naked, without weapons to defend myself. I have, besides surviving and feeding myself, to search for my internal path of perfection.'

Jeremy smiles happily when remembering his youthful trail.

- I do not change my experiences for anything in the world, he continues.

'During your walking you do think you are alone. Only when you attain your goal, and after you report all you encounters, the elders ask such a quantity of questions that you perceive them constantly watching you.'

'But, that is at the end.'

'I, like all, first got myself, in a eucalyptus forest, a small and perfect looking tree from the outside.'

'I hit it smoothly and listened if its inside was emptied by termites.'

I cut it, refined its two extremes, with a tender branch I made a knot to load it in my shoulder, I wrapped up one edge, filled it with water, closed the other cavity.'

'The 'didgeridoo' is my symbol as it represents me. It accompanies me in my walking, and afterwards, with it, I sing my history.'

'But before I vocalize in front of you, consent for me to recount a little about my moves.'

Jeremy speaks with a deep and loud voice, holding it, so not to shout in front of the public. His words, scarce and limited, are opposite of those of an orator. They break in on, back out to explain something not said before, and when translating a psychic experience, lived in another language, he grafts an unknown vocabulary.

The group becomes a little impatient with him because they want to listen to a short didgeridoo play, and the artist takes a long time in introducing his song.

- When you are naked under this great sun, continues Jeremy, you find yourself really impotent, and you begin to see the world that surrounds you in a different way: the plants, that you could care less about before, manifest themselves to you, as new, in front of your eyes.

'And you do begin the task of observing.'

'You had seen them previously. Now you penetrate in their essence, and they reveal to you their curative or nourishment qualities.'

'The animals, when perceiving them, are manifested as forms of vital strength. They become indicators of your progress.'

'The first animal I saw in my exit was a little bird, very common in Australia. I observed many of them in my advancement, and they always indicated me to search among the smallest, the imperceptible, or the humble entities, my ascending road.'

'When I wanted to eat meat, I had to kill. If it wanted to swallow fish I had to trawl.'

'These animals, when consumed, became part of me.'

'The old Australian continent was divided before in more than 300 nations, with even other 700 languages and dialects.'

'For thousands of years nobody moved a stone to usurp foreign territory.'

'When entering one of them, I had to identify myself, and ask permission, and, all of them, pleasantly, offered it to me.'

'So as I reached the snow-covered and cold mountains I proposed myself in my walk.'

'I found other human beings, with a similar language, but different.'

'I also found my wife.'

'This youthful path is a Way of self discovery.'

'I do manifest myself, get out of my obscurity, or closet, when I observe the whole creation and relate with it. Animals, plants, people, when observing them, I perceive what it is in me and discover myself.'

'My walk must be soft, so no one perceives it, but me; and I leave no vestige, so my steps remain unnoticed.'

'I develop, specially, the art of finding water in arid conditions, and search for hidden sources.'

'In the springs, I must discover the Rainbow Snake, living in the depth of the cavities of water.'

'Months later, I returned to my place of origin to report my deeds, to sing, with my own lyrics, my deep mysteries.'

'And in here is where I got to speak about the didgeridoo. Not only it serves to load water, I engage into leaving it wither to dry in order that it sounds well, because this trunk of eucalyptus is my voice, the instrument of my internal Word.'

'It is through it that we narrate our terrestrial walking and our adventures, the plants, the animals, the humans, the pure breathing of the mountains, the heavy inhaling of the deep valleys, the aridness of the desert without waters, the Sun burning each cell of your being, this nakedness so brilliant and supremely great. When you reach puberty and of all your senses, all of your body opens to the creation and you appreciate in each breath of air, in every drop of water, the multiple colors of creation: your hands caress; your ears listen to the constant song not only of nature, but of the whole universe; your eyes discover starry nights that move you to future humanities; your nose smells the most varied perfumes; your taste opens to different flavors, discovering an endless variety in the same tree.'

'I am telling you of something that you have not even the most remote idea. I am not criticizing you in absolute. Simply I am referring you to my world, an earth you cannot understand, because your culture had blocked your perception.'

'You have covered yourselves with clothing, and you have prevented your extra-sensorial awareness, and the only fact you've got within your reach is a mental knowledge of how to survive and make money in your cities.'

'But you do not know a thing of the Life in me, nor the joy satisfying my heart.'

'You do think, because I got not possessions, I am defenseless; and precisely is the opposite. Your wealth only covers the impotence of your bodies, stridden along by you to all vital observation.'

'And it appears to me such an absurdity as the one you've got as owning an instrument to reach the Divinity, and you do stun it with external sweepings, refusing its use, as a tool to attain God.'

'Pardon my intrusion. It was not, I say it again, motivated by bitterness or envy, but by the desire of sharing my Way and our Aboriginal culture.'

'I am threading you, not a pretty history that you could remember with the delight of your ears. What I testify is my life.'

'My Life.'

'The Didgeridoo symbolizes my visible body.'

'A body characterized as a stick.'

'A stick that is empty.'

Emptiness in need to be cleaned with water.'

'Water hidden, not only in creation, but also within myself.'

'A concealed spot from where it flows, not only the Water of rebirth, but a Wind penetrating and renovating, flowing in a lively spring and sprouting, revitalizing my spirit.'

'This spirit, air or wind, is not mine, but belongs to the commonwealth of creation.'

'And for an instant, when in flowing through my empty stick, the Wind takes a form: the shape of the Rainbow Snake. It is a wind with infinity of colors, not physical, but spiritual. The Rainbow is that Air Snake penetrating me, and becoming visible in my body. This one is the Way of Truth and of Life.'

'It is an airy and humid Strength, because the light of the Sun is in need of the air and of the water to show itself. It is a hidden energy springing up from the abyss, climbing to the highest point of the sky, and returning to the earth to fecundate it anew.'

'It is the energy of the stars manifested in my.'

'And this air is my voice, that flowing through the didgeridoo communicates my internal Word to the whole creation.'

'And I learned an extremely difficult skill, that is, to inhale this air and exhale at the same time. This is the Aboriginal technique producing an unbroken sound through which I describe my walk and my encounters.'

'And I do not sing only for my audience. I want to direct my hum but to the stars, to humanities waiting for my redemption.'

He continued explaining about the didgeridoo being an instrument assisting us to express what is in our hearts.

- Listen carefully; if I direct myself to the mountain, my sound has a different dictation to the one it has if I lead myself to the valley. Do try to penetrate, beyond the voice, into the eternal Word flowing trough me.

Jeremy continues teaching the difference between sounds, trying to help the audience in their self-discovery, to achieve a personal nakedness, without fear, with an absolute freedom, to face the Light.

I, since Jeremy began his presentation, could not hold up myself anymore, and what comes out from me is weeping and sobbing, with an emotion so enormous, as the one somebody gets, when reaching his purpose, attaining his goal.

Those, whom my mind refused as uncultivated, reveal to me the end of my evolution.

And in one of those instants when Life shares itself with us, I understand 'Unity'.

All humanity is breathing the same air, penetrating, without making distinction, not only inside the people, but also animals, plants and stones, even the deepest of our being, bursting the internal source, that particle of God, we all carry inside.

The human being, represented in the didgeridoo, is not a sexual or asexual organism. The 'I' stick standing for the male and 'U' characterizing the woman, are not sexual organs.

The human being is a channel open from top to bottom with air, a musical instrument where the Word of God resounds.

The Kundalini, Feathered Snake, Rainbow Snake, the standing Snake fabricated by Moses in the desert, is an ethereal and aquatic energy, that has to be erected on a stick to be seen.

And when you observe it, it becomes your companion.

Your sight, when discovering it, generates your own spiritual awakening.

And in this unique dot I discovered my puberty and my encounter with thousands of human beings.

And all my spiritual evolution comes to me concentrated in an instant, and the words of the Teacher resound, new, in my ether:

- You no longer belong to the lower world...

- I have pulled you up from that world...

- The Air, the Spirit, will reveal to you the complete Truth...

- You will weep and cry in your search, while the world laughs... but your sorrow will become joy.

- You will walk alone, but won't be unaccompanied, because the Father is with you...

- The Father will keep you; He will consecrate and protect you in your walk...

- You will be expelled from everywhere...

- They will condemn you to death for being who you are... thinking they are giving cult to God...

-I am the grapevine... My Father is the grape grower... He cuts off the dry branches... He prunes the healthy one so it may produce more fruit...

- If you do not unite yourselves to my Spirit, you could not accomplish anything...

- If this lower world hates you, know that it also has hated me first...

- You have not chosen me. I have selected you...

- I say it to you before it takes place, so when it happens you will know I had told you so...

- Now I call you 'Friend'...

- Like the Father loves me, so I love you...

- Live in my Love...

- This is my only instruction: Love all your brothers...

Jeremy blows through the didgeridoo and its deep sound, penetrating through my feet, destroys the high pitch of the apocalyptic trumpets, creating a New

Heaven.

Burning tears of joy, it floods my extremities.

I observe my feet. The two of them guided me on my pilgrimage. They, in the Bible, represent the soul.

- Wash your feet, one another...

And Jeremy, with his song, rinses my feet, purifies me so I enter into a New Heaven. My tears are so abundant, and I feel such a fool, that I search for, in the darkness, a corner to hide in.

I am the last one going out, and, still with ignited eyes, I direct myself to Jeremy:

- I have no words to thank you for the great deal you initiated in me today.

- Not, thanks to you for allowing me to teach you, he says repeating the same words of Kathy.

- May I embrace you? I ask him.

- I am a married man and I have two daughters and a son, he responds.

- I only want to embrace you, I insist.

- It is all right, he answers.

THIRD INSERT FROM THE SPIRIT

I
A name I call
MYSELF
Name of God in the Bible:
I AM

I

What happened to me that people could not understand my point of view?

Some human beings hold in their inside Word, they thrum my soul and their poetry snatches my breath, revealing my essence.

The Word of Jeremy boosts me to the Firmament and immediately, when asking him for an embrace so my love would calm down with the touch, his same voice refuses me as useless.

- Do you understand something? My own I questions me.

Which you have written has not crossed your understanding. You have to reread it all over again, meditate on it and analyze it.

The book you have written is not for others but for yourself.

You are trying to reach my spirit, but it is impossible to attain perfect knowledge.

I express myself in all as I pierce it all.

Each pebble speaks to you of me, as it does each small leaf or flower or animal or human being.

God doesn't make any distinction between peoples or amid creation.

How is God to prefer a fruit to another fruit, or a human being beneath another? The One, who watches with the same love, the eagle hovering on the ether and the worm hiding buried, how is He not to observe equally all human beings?

How do you want them to comprehend you, if you, craving for your spiritual nakedness, only worry about the appearances, and you do respect the monk for his saffron tunic and annul the great teaching of Klahan?

You want them to understand you and you still ignore me, the one now talking to you.

It is I, the one verbalizing in Klahan, in the monk, in Jeremy... in all and in each particle of creation.

It is none other than I. Listen to my words and pay attention. And don't make distinction between people. Imitate the Almighty in His Love.

You don't need to go all over the world searching for a universal religion of the spirit. That is just a vain thought.

You are really what Jeremy communicated: an empty shaft, without viscera or heart, to the one beaten smoothly until it opens, to become an air instrument, so my spirit could flow through it and communicate with creation.

And you accompany me to the height and to the depth, because I pierce it all, and I enter in you and I get out of you without asking your permission, because you are only my instrument, but I am.

The daughter of the Lin family has been the most accurate one. God doesn't want any offerings or sacrifices: He has given you a body.

And in this body you work so I may flow better through it. Your food has to be air. Your drink: wind with water.

What I want from you is to keep a perfect instrument. And the excellence is as much internal as external.

The uniqueness I want in you is your body, your cover.

Look! Do an experiment, since it pleases you so much:

I want a flower, or better yet, the color of a flower.

Imagine a red rose, and try to take away its tint. What remains are a few transparent petals.

In the same way, what I want from you is your dye. The special distinctiveness enchanting me is your skin. And you must lay it under the Sun, so the supreme star may pack it with colors.

Now, moreover, with tanning problems and solar spots, so common, because you humans have wasted already this beautiful planet, my desire of redemption vanishes because I cannot find the colors I love in any skin.

But, I am talking to your spiritual understanding, not to a physical mind.

Search for that strong and powerful Sun, filtering your skin with colors, keep walking in the desert without water, under this burning star until your skin becomes black.

When will you understand me completely, you, wanting to be perceived?

All those you find in your way tell you about myself. But they articulate partially and without understanding. Therefore Kathy, Jeremy... and all, veiled, enlighten you.

But as their particle of Truth, just like yours, lacks meditation of the spirit, they offer you limited or partial teachings from their viewpoint.

Therefore the Teacher represents the Way in its most perfect form, and I am going to explain to you His words.

The Snake, the Rainbow one and all the rest, is the strength of the spirit.

Moses prophesied on that force, but

he did not carry it out, when placing it, in the desert, over your stick: symbol of healing for the ones who see it.

She is the same Teacher, nailed on the wood, so all could perceive the instability, anarchy and depth of the spirit.

I am telling you the Snake doesn't return to the lower worlds to regain power, neither ascends to the infinite Universe.

They have removed, with its crucifixion, its deepness and volatility.

It only keeps its internal anarchy, naked under a burning Sun.

And in this disturbance it revolts against all it finds, because the aversion to its crucifixion has caused an anarchical love towards the whole Universe.

And in there, nailed to the cross, the Son of Man, meaning all of what you have begotten and produced with your stick, without moving, quiet and static, begins to ascend to the Infinite.

That one is Love.

That one is the Love of the Father.

That one is the color the Father wants to extract from you: that black and so attractive Light containing the millions of colors of all creation.

- Watch out! I am the one talking to you.

I Am.

I Am spirit, you are mind.

I Am the Way; you are the instrument with the one I make my entrance.

I Am the Truth; you are a carnal body where the Truth resounds.

I Am the Door; you are the one that has to come to the portico.

I Am a Beautiful and Good spirit, you are coarse matter in search for beauty.

I Am the Life; you are destruction because you are death.

I know; you are searching for wisdom.

I desire loneliness and you crave for company.

You want them to understand you, but you are at where you are at, not so they may hear you, but as a result you may understand.

You want to know the Truth, but I give the orders, and I don't want to communicate to you my Truth because I know it would harm you greatly.

You have begun to write this book to help your childhood friend. Do you think you are helping him?

It is possible it could be 'yes', or it is probable it might be 'not'.

But these have not to be of your concern.

Your desire of serving, that one is the

energy you need for your own development.

This avidity has taken you to search for, in your notes of travel, memories that could be of interest to your friend.

And it has been I, the one that, using these evocations, have manifested to you. My truth has been revealed in multiple excerpts. And it continues exposing constantly; at every moment, with each one of the people, animals, plants and as much as objects there are in the creation, in order that, each second, you may continue being nourished and manifested by my spirit.

But your mind has not noticed your internal labor.

And I want that to be so.

I can only give you small tokens so your understanding may not expand in its labor, but continue glued to the physical.

You cannot live, as a being of flesh, in the realm of the spirit. You need to be there, in your position, tied to your work, because in this fixation, my spirit works.

You don't need to move. It is I the one shifting, traveling, walking. You are in there, on that evenness of earth, to be cautious of your body.

And, attending your organism, you feed my spirit, and I study in you, accumulating pigments and shades, until reaching the total burn.

Those are of no use, probably, to your friend, nor to anybody else in the world, but to you.

And if you find only a human being to share them, then your work already has been fulfilled.

Your main duty is to bring out to the surface, with your song, my essence, which is air, which is spirit.

And when this breath of yours communicates with another lungful of air, produces a light so intense in this psychic reality in which I live, that benefits all the great community of the humanity.

And I extract from you that black light, which it is the union of millions of colors.

For you it is black, but when altering in spirituality it becomes transformed in white.

For you is dark, because, seeing with your carnal eyes, it represents the absence of light, the nothingness, the vacuum, the obscurity, the death.

But when transmuted, it is transfigured in 'All', in the 'pleroma' or totality, in Light, in Life.

But you continue being an empty trunk, an instrument I use to manifest myself, a piece of flesh dying when the spirit gives up.

For you the death is the end, the vacuum, the nothingness, the obscurity, the not being.

But you are death, because you may not transform yourself along with your soul.

And I, from this level, have to kill you, once and again, and prepare your reincarnation, all over again, immaculate, until your perception, shut in itself from the beginning of the creation, may open to the breath and recognize that I am the one giving the guidelines, the one who knows it all.

And, when you get to be my perfect instrument, I come down from my heights and acquire your obscurity, blackness and death, and take you near me, because neither the obscurity, nor the blackness, or the death exists: they are simply creations of your imagination, with its atrocious fear of the Infinite, to be lost and to become naked.

For me, all this work, that for you looks useless, is valuable, because in your blackness and obscurity you are illuminating and guiding me for all the Eternity.

And do you know how important this is?

You have understood nothing of the book, but have reached the goal.

You neither have written it.

I have been the author and I have thought it, if only for one spiritual being, that may read between the lines and find the spirit.

What lacks now is for you to surrender your physical body, as an offering to the Creator, so it may mold what you due to others.

And remember, you would only pay a tiny fraction of your debt.

As John, offer your body as victim, because that one is the law of the Creator.

Once I extract my colors, I no longer need you, and I must abandon you.

You will think I throw you away with contempt, but it is not so.

In your rejection and forsakenness, I will be always with you because I love you.

I loved you knowing you as my enemy and now, moreover, I thank you for your offering. Thanks to you I have received my Light and my everlasting Life.

Don't wait for praises for your letters nor for my Word. The human mind always will refuse them poking between lines to discover the vital organs. But it will never get it.

The book is useful to you.

Analyze what in it is written, and never stop, nor for an instant, absorbing my air, my spirit and this will keep you firm in your transmutation.

THE BAPTISM

The leftovers of the exterior hurricane reflected my psychic state, remembering ancient rejections. The low atmospheric pressure pushed me to the darkest depths of my being.

When getting out of the car, the rain soaked me completely.

I arrive at the reception, and the clerk referred me immediately to the secretary of the Boss, and without delay I could listen to the strong treads of her heels.

- Come in! She said with her bitter and unaffectionate face, trying to force a smile, and showing a grimace.

She led me to a waiting room, sumptuously decorated, so my poverty could register the power the Boss has over his subjects.

I would not gaze over the luxurious furniture trying to flatten my innocence, but I observed what these objects could hide.

And so, I noticed the dust of the corners, the dirtiness dissembled behind the sofa, the marks of a coffee cup on the small table, a torn down image.

I went towards the statuette, with my handkerchief I erased the dust, arranged it, and afterwards I lounged on the sofa, contemplating the cloud of dust on the carpet.

The German language has a beautiful word: 'gemüt', designating the placidness the soul feels in certain places. For me, in these moments, I qualify the waiting room as 'gemüt-lish', without soul gentleness.

- The Boss will receive you now, the secretary says from the door of the waiting room.

I've been delayed twenty-two minutes.

- Come on! The Boss said with kindness.

- You are cold, he indicated as soon as I tend him my hand.

I wanted to tell him I was not cold, but dead, but my lips could not open.

- Remove your jacket, because you are all wet, he adds immediately.

And I, so cherishing my spiritual nakedness, on asking me to discover in front of him, I answered him:

- Thanks Boss, but not. I am fine as it is.

- Sit down! He prompted branding a

chair.

His Assistant was seated, static, on another stool, and with a head gesture indicated me to sit down and fixing that the meeting would be brief and bitter.

- It has reached my ears, that you don't like the Ministers; the Boss said, following the dictation of his Assistant, with a mellow tone, affecting an internal ache.

Really, I reflected at once, I have never tasted any of them, and I don't know what flavor they hold and, only the idea of sinking my teeth into anointed flesh, disgusts me.

- And who has informed you so? I ask.

- I have my secret sources, and cannot indicate them to you, he answers.

- Hum! I refuse, because they have informed you wrong.

- To me, the received information is the correct, so gather all your things and leave. I don't want to see you again.

At that same instant, I listen to the voice of my father, inciting me from the distance of my childhood, with hardness and constrain:

- Coward! Fight!

- The courage is not to clash face to face, I allege in my inside, but to hold up the fury of the hate, to protect us with the shield of Love, and resist the blow of those who want my destruction, and use the treachery to execute it.

'Jesus, I continue in my inside, praying, I already know that You are not here, and You do not even enter into this building, but, just in a case there is somebody over there listening, and could be of interest, I say to You the following:

- I am not fighting. I am here to lend a hand to those who want to be helped.

'But what there is in me, or what I could give them, nobody wants it, not the Boss, neither his Assistant, nor anyone else, not even my father. They do not understand me, nor lean on me.'

'So be it, I have lost my life studying for something that doesn't exist.'

'You are of interest to nobody.'

'Everyone hold their believes in the institutions, in the Boss, and they get to think the corporations are those saving them, not You.'

'They could not understand me, but neither have they heard You.'

'Now that I find myself as lonely, and thrown away as trash, I feel closer to You.'

'Already we could say the two of us, by accident, are together.'

'What a failing of a lifetime and what uselessness of humanity we hold as eternal brothers.'

'From where I am, I see neither God, nor anybody up there, or light. I could not identify from where comes so much hate. I don't know who planted those seeds of violence in our society.'

'I wish death would be certain, and I remained here, disappearing forever, so no one could remember that I was born.'

'I find myself so impotent in front of so many enemies hating me.'

'And why am I telling it to You if You do not listen?'

'Complete by now all this farce; throw me to the forgotten junk.'

'Until here I come with my priesthood: 'You are priest forever according to the rite of Melchisedech', and with title and all, it doesn't has any value.'

'I have failed.'

'Or better yet, You do not succeed, because it is You the one they neither understand, nor want it to; no one cares for anything: neither your Way, nor your thinking.'

'They have invented a religion with doubtful virgins and mud saints and prayers, moving little tiny pieces of plastic, one after another.'

'Ha, ha, ha... I have pity for this pile of human flesh, destined to be slaughtered and driven to the pain of the unconsciousness, day after day criticizing and hating others, and refusing to look at them.'

'What You must invent is a mirror, and place it in front of each human being.'

'Stare to what Cervantes suggested in 'Don Quixote': the Gentleman of the Mirrors. That is what You have to innovate, somebody has to place a mirror in front of Don Quixote, in front of the spirit, in order that the person could glaze, may contemplate himself from above, notice his erroneous actions, and could get under the management of Sancho Panza, of the belly, because they only think about eating, but the ideals are dead in our society.'

'How wrong have You done it all. And I call you 'Teacher', and your wisdom is not profitable. You have failed even more than me.'

'So, here you have it, take your Priesthood, thanks for it all, but I do not need you. If You don't even listen to me, why do I keep talking to You? Am I demented, speaking to myself?'

Suddenly I perceive with my spirit an image: I am a tiny grain of sand in the base of an urn. Three heels: the three persons plotting my destruction, become cruel against the insignificant particle of sand,

and with force, the trio in unison, flatten me.

In their fury, they have occasioned a split of openness in the vase, and all the sand in the container emerges, first, slowly, lately, with time, increases in speed, until the vessel remains completely empty.

To me, to the tiny particle of sand, they could not destroy. How could it be ruined with the fragileness and fatness of the flesh, the efficiency and essence of the spirit?

When descrying the tiny orifice, I find a little excerpt of Light, and proceed to the exit.

- Not you! The Teacher says, securing me with his hand, smoothly and with lots of Love.

'You cannot go out until all are absent. You will be the last one to leave.'

- So, I return again to what I was saying before, I answer trying to join the previous vision with the earlier conversation, I am not fighting. You resolve it to your likeness, because I am not doing a thing.

- I need to leave to see if someone is in need of help, the Assistant says suddenly.

The Boss and I remain seated, amazed over the action of the Assistant.

The Boss throws me out of work. I am fixed in my seat, enclosed in an internal dialogue, of which they, apparently, know nothing. What I reported happened in a few short seconds. And the walking out of the Assistant leaves the Boss more perplexed that myself. For me, it is an answer to my vision.

I remained seated in front of the Boss. We do not know what to say to each other.

He bends his head as a sign of tiredness.

I look at him to see if I find some conscience beyond the appearances.

Another vision emerges in my soul.

This time, it is opposite.

I am the Boss, in Germany, and they have brought to me a French citizen, that I throw boldly and pitilessly from the corporation.

What takes place now is a copy of something previous, with inverted characters.

- Poor fellow, I say inwardly to the Boss seated in front of me.

'Your wickedness has taken you only to be Boss, I, with my malice, moved higher; I whisper in my inside, with an arrogance and nastiness coming out of my memory.'

'What a horrible individual I have been.'

'I already want to leave out of here, as badly as the Boss could treat me, I do not pay, not even, ten per cent of what I did to him.'

'I treated him with much perversity, how diabolical I am, how much wickedness I find still in me. How merciless I was.'

- Boss, I say profoundly, act as you want that I will never criticize you. You are much more merciful with me of than I was with you.

'I don't judge you for what you do, or for what others oblige you to proceed. Now I Love you, and from here I ask your pardon, for the huge wrongdoings I did to you in the past.'

- The person in charge could not be found, it says the Assistant entering the office, they are trying to locate him and we have to wait a few minutes.

He sits again, and we all stay quiet, without daring anybody to pronounce a word, or to breathe.

In less of a minute, the Assistant straightens up again:

- I am going to call, to see if they have got a hold of him.

- All that happens in life, I continue with my inside reflection, it is a cancellation of something we owe.

'And we do not pay back, not even, the ten percent of what corresponds to us.'

'The parable of the Father, forgiving

all the debt; and the debtor demanding another defaulter the full cent per cent of all, plus the interests; it is a history we repeat incessantly.'

'I want them to give me the cent per cent of all, but I am annoyed when they ask me to repay only the ten per cent of my debt.

'I am not now reimbursing not even the ten per cent. We do not refund anything. We are as John the Baptist, which being Elijah decapitated five hundred bad priests, but he was beheaded only once.'

'If this is so, how wrongly did I behave in past, how much obscurity and hate I transmitted into society, when I see so many abhorring me.'

'Only You are Good, Father, when, amid the distress obstructing our life, You still do enlighten and encourage me in each one of them. What kindness is so great in You, that nor for a second leave us abandoned and forsaken.'

'With how much kindness You do link our lives, what fineness in Your hands on presenting us, with love, enemies and friends, encouraging us all to continue our painful walk.'

'You are pure Light, Father of the Stars, and with Your Word You open, chapter after lesson, the eternal history of our souls, so we could remember the purpose we made already thousands of years ago, and that we forget with so much frequency.'

'What it happens to me is repayment of what I owe and I only redeem myself when conscience of the wrong they do to me and, as fine alchemist, transmute it into good.'

'From my total abandonment, my very Beloved Teacher, I understand that 'To Love our enemy' is the most sublime principle of perfection. Because our enemies of today, have been our long forgotten friends, we are those who, first, have despised and betrayed them.'

'Now I understand You better. The vision of my past, that gift so beautiful, it is to pardon, to Love, to continue Loving, with a True Love, to all those beings we have relegated to the obscurity of hate, and only through our Love, they could wake up to a new life.'

'From the depth of the abandonment of my soul I ask You, Teacher, to give me strength to work constantly in the common good, loving my enemies and giving them all of what they ask from me; because, although it appears me to be a lot of, is not even a tiny fraction of what I owe them.'

- Teach me how you do what you are

conceiving, the voice of the Boss tells me, penetrating my inside, sharing in my secret conversation.

- They cannot find him, says the Assistant, just in that instant when entering again the administrative center.

- Then, it muttered the Boss, go out to wherever you want to, and I will call you if I need you.

- Uf! is my only answer, bending my head.

And I went out running to the car. The sun shone with all its strength through the dark clouds. I removed my wet jacket. I drove until my house. I undress and completely naked, plunged into the swimming pool.

- My Friend, I pronounce in the loneliness around me, here I am, next to You, as You are, naked, fixed in my work and trying to follow Your steps.

'Today I have reached the total nakedness. I have seen the wickedness still in me and the great Love I must share with all of humanity. How lonely I find myself! I am so abandoned and relegated that I discover myself Free and Happy. Why do I have so much Love towards all those incompetent people?'

'What Love so huge You have when You call us Brothers; how far away are we to be called worthy of God, His children.'

'Thanks, Father, because in each action of our life facilitate the opportunity of transcending this lower world, and cross over to the reality You already have prepared for us.'

'What a sublime approach You have arranged, and no one can neither upset nor move it.'

'Thanks, Beloved Teacher, for instructing me at every moment. Do not abandon me in this dark crucifixion of the lower worlds, and give me strength to search always in me for the pardon of my enemies and the Love towards all the creation.'

Naked in the spirit, my body feels abandoned and rejected.

I plunge into the water, and extend my arms in form of a cross. I want to enlarge them, and hatch the whole world in an embrace of Love. I wish to drink the sea, and absorb in me the whole water of creation.

And I observe each cell of my body, all the millions of them soaked with water. Starving and sad, they have being all day without feeding. But, with it all, they are happy. They find themselves renewed with the purifying bath. They have accompanied me for many existences, on some of them, the blows felt very harsh, others have enjoyed the flavor of the fruits, but each one of them has taken part in every one of the life experiences.

I do not need to drink the sea anymore; I have enough with a drop of water.

And, still below the water, I observe each one of these, my cells, absorbing a molecule of water, a minimal fraction of the terrestrial wealth.

My cells have found the Door of access to the world of the spirit, and each one of them, tries to untie from the others, to transcend, alone, to a new level, and in there be repaired to form a new body.

But not, the water keeps them assembled, agglutinated, without any possibility of outdoing the matter.

John the Baptist appears in front of me and I smile to see him next to me, synthesizing, in a second, all my terrestrial pilgrimage.

The bath He started, acquires cosmic dimensions.

The water is the element of creation sticking together all the living cells among themselves, impeding their escape evasion from this physical world, forcing an attraction towards the depth of the matter, towards the elements more low and despised, and promoting, on that precipice, the humbleness, purity and chastity of their nature.

And all cells smile with joy when knowing them assemble and humble, recovering their original chastity and purity.

And when ransom them; a particle of air, of spirit, comes out of every one of them.

It is the same water, the one that, in the lowland, produces the air of the spirit.

And the air, when coming out, becomes steam and this one develops into fire.

And the Divine arrangement is so perfect, that my eyes, when contemplating it, weep of happiness. And with their sobbing underwater join the remainder of the cells, and illustrate their internal air and fire, observing that the earth, the water, the air and the fire are one.

The water is the only element uniting the other three.

And the Teacher joins us, with a smile extremely beautiful, so stunning it kills my heart.

I am experiencing the baptism of fire. The water of John is not the one extinguishing the fire of the Teacher; on the contrary, from it the fire sprouts, and the water is the one that begets life.

I am no longer myself. The Father and I are one.

This flame of alive Love, eternally blazing, it is a new purification, burning all it finds.

The expulsion of the systems, and this new burning in the quietness of the water, has produced my Ascension.

Already I see the Earth from a superior world. The Orient and West rub against each other, but I admire the African continent like a great heart.

The water of the Jordan leads me to the Red Sea.

I don't ask God to open the waters so I could go through as Moses did.

I retrace the walking of the ancient people of Israel, but this time I want to plunge into the Red Sea fire, and I wish for its waters to cover me with crimson.

And I enter the burning desert of the African heart, divided in four compartments.

Africa becomes the continent of Redemption for all humanity.

And following the advice of the Egyptian Initiates, I direct myself to the lower left ventricle, in which is found the 'Sperma Logos', the essence of the Divinity.

But, since I left the Jordan, I enter a magnificent world, totally inverted, on the other side of the mirror.

And I find the lower left ventricle in the Pyramid.

When entering in Egypt all the gods crash into dust. The material world decomposes to my steps.

The Almighty God, the Father of the Stars, from a distance of light years, observes me lovingly.

The whole Universe contemplates me, and the four fixed points of Aquarius,

Leo, Taurus and Scorpio, transmit a ray of light, lining up a cross, whose center is the Sphinx, that with cautious penetrating eyes differs my existence.

- I am only a human being, another one from the crowd. I have taken conscience of my dignity as child of God, and here I am, vagabond, transiting to the house of my Father.

And I enter into the Pyramid.

John and the Teacher contemplate me. They have being with me since the beginning. The two hierophants don't aid me anymore with potions in order that I could find my route.

They simply observe my action.

The Egyptian Initiatrix Chamber it opens for me. It is a tomb of light.

My emotion is so huge, that the annihilation of my human body could not stop it.

The weeping of fire continues flooding with water the resting place where I find myself.

I am dying of Love.

And I enter, first the feet, later the body; but when I attempt to settle my head, this one doesn't subsist anymore; I do not hold any thought in me.

I have found the Door of access to a new world.

Weeping of joy, with this burning fire, the cells glow giving up their material shed, ascending to another superior existence.

I have discovered the Way.

I listen to the Word of the Teacher:

- I am the Door
- I am the Way

And the Way is not either Christian, or atheistic, or it goes to the human heart, or to the infinite, neither to the home of the Father. The Way is. I am the Way.

It is walking that we advance, but we don't move. I delayed behind so much because I entertain a lot, thinking the Way went to the House of the Father, or to other place, or to the human heart, and I consider thinking what to take, how to walk, ascertaining other views of what was waiting for me in the future.

And the Way doesn't go anywhere, but produces an attitude in the soul, of keeping oneself relegated in the periphery of the society, next to the despised, and rejected.

I took long in learning that the Way is what is the important. Not the destiny, or the style of walking, but the Way: that razor's edge, wounding your soul, destroying, despising and denying you until makes of you a vagabond: without residence or destiny, making friends in this walking and leading you towards the Almighty God.

- You have wept while the world around you laughed, notices the Teacher, but your sadness will become sheer joy.

'When transcending from one level to another, it all inverts, and just as the water, united with air, produces the steam and the steam develops into fire, incinerating it all, returning to the earth; the water, when bonding the other three elements, is not eliminated, but it is transformed. The earth, fire and air are all united in the water.'

'What it occurs in the creation, it happens inside you.'

'This water, with the air of your spirit, has produced tears of happiness or laments of grief, that it doesn't matter; what it transcends are the sobs, so hot, they burn more than fire; and in their transformation they had incinerated you completely, returning your body to the earth on which it was born.'

'But the water has not disappeared, simply it has transformed you. Your body, which you have used for many lives, has been formed out of cells and substances located in this planet.'

'But your body does not belong to you. It is a dress that you have to return to the Creator of this material reality.'

'The organism has assisted you in your transformation. The water, inside you, has transmuted, and has transfigured you with it.'

'Now, when seeing your dust inside the coffin, you observe another condition. That one aquatic configuration you don't need it anymore. It only can be used here.'

'But, in this threshold of the new world, you cannot employ it as instrument; you must return it to the earth from where it comes from.'

'Now you do not posses a body, your buried remains wait, again, for the humbleness of the water to be reborn.'

'And they will be taken, once more, by another human being, that, one by one, he will compile and articulate until forming a perfect Being, that will discard them, when he abandons the matter to become pure soul.'

'These cells, this water, neither can it be manufactured, nor it can be extinguish, it is the gift of this blue azure planet, a reflection of the divinity, that, through it, relieves all of creation.'

'All the beings crossing through the

Earth use it: we drink it, expel it out from our organism, again we swallow it and dirty it, but it returns again to its original humbleness, pure and chaste, and it teaches all of us to join in this process.'

'After a long time, these cells that you have used and discarded, when developing, will become also pure souls.'

'Therefore the care of the body is the only pleasant sacrifice to the Almighty, loving each one of these cells, cleaning them, nourishing them with live elements: this one is the donation to God. He does not want either offerings or holocausts, but has given us a body.'

'In this new level, your mind remains burned in the grave, and you do not hold a particle of dust in your being, you are simply Light.'

'Welcome home.'

'Still you are not trained for this total reality of light, but: Observe!'

I investigate between the dusk and with lots of Love reveals Guty, in his hands a white tunic folded that, solemnly, unfolds and imposes upon me.

- Now you are a priest forever according to rite of Melchisedech, he asserts.

Luminous Essences cover, with a slab of stone, my remains in the Egyptian tomb, preparing an altar.

The bread and the wine represent the whole work and the human effort.

- Offer to God, insinuates Guty, a liturgy as it should be done.

The Baptist places a drop of water in the chalice, on the wine.

The Altar book is open to the left. Without mouth, neither sound, my eternal Word flows, changing neither punctuation nor accent.

The Word becomes Life.

The Life turns out to be Light for all the humanity.

It could be found on Earth and all was created through it.

We men did not recognize it.

When we recognize it, it gives us internal strength to become Children of God Almighty

And so, as Melquisedec, without father or mother, lacking beginning or end of days, I lift up my hands with the dish of bread and with the chalice of wine and water.

Blessed are You God Almighty
For this bread and this wine
Fruit of this Earth
And of human labor

I am celebrating the Mass of the Ascension, and I continue reading in the Preface:

Today is the day when Our Lord
Ascended gloriously to the most high of heavens
Between the acclamations of higher Beings
He has not gone to abandon us
But to raise up to heavens the fallen human nature
When seeing Him entering, the full firmament bursts out with joy...
And we, here in the depth, blend our voices to theirs singing:
Holy, Holy, Holy is the Lord
God of the Universe
The Heavens and the Earth are filled with your Glory

Hosanna in the Firmament
Blessed is the one who comes in the name of the Lord

I read slowly, Word after diction, and every one of them acquires life on being broadcasted by the spirit:

We ask you, Almighty Father...
To grant us Peace
To protect us in our Way
You bring us together in Unity...
With your holy Apostles:
Peter, Paul,

When pronouncing their name, their spirits turn present.

The great Paul manifests just as he was in the past, with the Jewish Thelma on his shoulders. The first one who understood the Teacher smiles with lots of love when been called. But, immediately, he steps back, returning to the shade. He communicates, without pronouncing a sound:

- I did not was called by the Teacher to be part of the Twelve.

I notice the Canon so perfect, it has imperfections.

...and Andrew

The apostles arrive two by two.

James and John

Each apostle, when mentioned, takes his position around the Altar. The Teacher convokes them to be the Twelve Doors of entrance to the Heavenly Jerusalem.

Thomas and James
Philip and Bartholomew
Matthew and Simon

Ahead of me is shaping a New Heaven.

I have neither tears nor eyes, but I want to continue weeping with emotion and I could not.

I find myself between Heaven and Earth, in front of the only Door of access to the Father of the Stars.

Thaddeus

Jude Thaddeus has been left alone, without companion.

I discover more imperfections in the Canon. Not only it had them since its origin, but these same imperfections are necessary, as they are in any good work of art, in order that beauty could be fully manifested.

Here, in the lower world, everything has to include faults; they are part of this reality. And when one wants to make it all perfect, it only produces such a sweetness that it pulls away the person who understands well.

Also the group of Twelve has a blemish, and the error is Jude Iscariot. But this gloom is necessary so the absolute fineness of the Teacher could be obvious. The treason of Judas becomes the best of the

Twelve Doors.

And I follow my reading adding:

.... *And Judas.*

And Judas comes in front of the Eleven. They that carried out so wrong with him, bend their heads, a little ashamed. Which Judas did for the Teacher, surpasses them all.

The Teacher smiles on seeing figured His salvation. Without the presence of Judas, the redemption would fail, because the Messiah is designated as 'Savior of the World'

And Judas smiles as if satisfied, watching his ancient companions and regaining a new dignity. His star becomes the most shining of the Twelve.

It is a new Heaven.

Accept this offering....
Of those reborn
From Water and Spirit
Forgiving all our mistakes...
Count us with your elects.
May from this instant on
My offering
Be perfect
Spiritual
Worthy of You
So that, for us, it could be
The Body
And the Blood

Of your beloved son Jesus Christ
Whom taking this bread He said
'Take and eat it, this is my body'
And taking this glorious Chalice,

The chalice I hold with my hands changes of shape. The container is not important, but the content.

The Chalice also is of Egyptian origin.

It symbolized the vestal matrix, which with the water unites the diversity of spiritual elements, preparing to give birth, to beget life for a new world.

This is the same Chalice He uses, the Holy Grail searched for by His followers.

It is a cup of air, a concave and ventilated vessel, where germinates a new life.

In his blessed and venerable hands

And I observe my hands, curved in, maintaining the wineglass, and are not my hands anymore, but is He, the Christ, sprouting from me, the one who embraces it.

Take and drink, this is my blood
Blood shared for all
For the forgiveness of sins

I Am the Bread and the Chalice, the food and the consumer, the matrix where coagulates the new existence and Life itself, priest and victim, giver and obtainer of the offering, receiving and emitting.

I Am male and female, but I am neither man nor woman; I am a new being, with life in itself. I Am Father and Mother.

I am the Light, the Truth, the Way, the Life, the Beauty, the Door, the Bread, the Wine, the Resurrection.

Do this remembering me.
This is the secret of our faith.

The voices of the faithful, from the background, answer with a routine assertion and without conviction. But their clamors, when resounding in the Pyramid, acquire life when revealing their own ascension:

We *announce your death*
We *proclaim your Resurrection*
Come Lord Jesus.

My diction continues giving out monotonously each syllable.

We *learn by heart Your glorious Death*
Your Resurrection
Your admirable Ascension...
Father do accept with kindness this offering
As you received Abel's offerings,
The sacrifice of Abraham,
And the bread and wine of Melchisedech

I am celebrating a Cosmic Mass, offering to God Almighty our painful wanderings in the abysmal depths of the lower world.

The Egyptian Initiates composed the

Canon; I do perceive them in the intimacy, experimenting, in the neophyte, the effects of their work.

Your holy martyrs
John the Baptist...

Here I find again my initiator, the lover of God, whom, with water, prepares our humanity for the instruction of the Teacher.

Matthias

Poor Matthias, been called by the Eleven to occupy the place of Judas, a door too huge for him.

But when he appears is full of joy, in his terrestrial paths, and with a lot of courage, has achieved to ascend until the height of Judas, and has become his beloved friend.

With his appearance, embraces Judas and settles to his side.

That's why the star of Judas shines so much, because it is a double star.

The Door of Judas opens to the Infinite; Judas and Matthias are the two lintels on in passing, the entrance and the exit towards a new Heaven, the union between John and the Teacher.

Nobody knew who the Messiah was, and Judas showed it: that one is his sin, his treason, but a necessary treachery and failing, because in this, our lower level, this one is the Law of the Father.

In the same way as Joseph, in the Old Testament, opened the Twelve Tribes of Jacob, and expanded, from Egypt, their irradiation throughout all the earth, in the same way comes Judas.

The children of Joseph: Ephraim and Manasseh, Jewish and Arab are the Egyptian Door of union between these two groups.

The imperfection of the Twelve is the perfection of the Law of the Father.

With each Word, my white tunic shows them, as in a film, my ascension to a new world.

But my Mass doesn't represent any human group: it is the offering of all the humanity.

And thousands of friends join me and enemies and traitors, all of them facilitated me to attain this fullness of the divinity in me, and so I don't catalog them as before. For me, already, all of them are one.

Yours is the Kingdom
Yours the Power
And the Glory
Our Father...
Let us share with one another our Peace.

And, without touching, we communicate a feeling of Peace, placing it on the Altar, so that, from here, it could irradiate to the whole creation.

And I split in two the round bread. I detach a tiny particle out from the lower left side, representing the 'Sperma Logos', and connect it to the wine and the water so it could generates a new life.

I superpose the two halves of the bread and to me it represents a ram with two horns. The symbol of evil appears on the dish, but I smile happily because wickedness subsists no more. The horns represent the two whirlwinds in opposition, and this time, the black hole, it is the brain, the mind of the ram.

Beyond the appearances of the ram, I see vaguely to Lamb of God, eradicating the Fall of the humanity.

I consume the bread and the wine. Wine that it is New. But I have neither physical body nor form; I am light assimilating intangible nutrition, which disappears immediately.

The Word finds the Silence.

Arcadia, Florida, USA 25 July 2006

INDEX

Prologue	3
Naked	9

First Canticle
Finding Freedom

The unknown person	13
Piquer	21
Semsem	29

Second Canticle
Unearthing springs of Living Waters

Lola	55
Lorraine	65
Vilma	77

Third Canticle
Coming across secret shelters

Madelyn and Del	89
Don José	109
"For Elisa" From Beethoven	117

Fourth Canticle
Attaining the Heart of Jesus

Dolores	129
The Teacher	135
Yairon	145

FIRST INSERT FROM THE SPIRIT

Manolo	163

SECOND INSERT FROM THE SPIRIT

Theo	179

Fifth Canticle
Gathering precious stones

Paco	193
The Group	201
Wai	209

Sixth Canticle
Getting high with wine

Steve	223
Family Lin	235
Hans and Rachel	245

Seventh Canticle
The Song of Songs

Bangkok
Guy	261
The Guide	264
Sunan	267
Klahan	277

Sydney
Kathy	285
Jeremy	291

THIRD INSERT FROM THE SPIRIT

I	305
The baptism	317

www.ingramcontent.com/pod-product-compliance
Lightning Source LLC
Chambersburg PA
CBHW032016230426
43671CB00005B/109